M000206074

coffee

100 everyday recipes

First published in 2012
LOVE FOOD is an imprint of Parragon Books Ltd

Parragon
Queen Street House
4 Queen Street
Bath BA1 1HE, UK

www.parragon.com/lovefood

ISBN: 978-1-4454-9875-1

Printed in China

Produced by Ivy Contract
Cover and new internal photography by Clive Streeter
Cover and new home economy and food styling by Angela Drake

Notes for the Reader

This book uses standard kitchen measuring spoons and cups. All spoon and cup measurements are level unless otherwise indicated. Unless otherwise stated, milk is assumed to be whole, butter is assumed to be salted, eggs are large, individual vegetables are medium, and pepper is freshly ground black pepper. Unless otherwise stated, all root vegetables should be washed and peeled before using.

For the best results, use a meat thermometer when cooking meat and poultry—check the latest USDA government guidelines for current advice.

Garnishes and serving suggestions are all optional and not necessarily included in the recipe ingredients or method. The times given are only an approximate guide. Preparation times differ according to the techniques used by different people and the cooking times may also vary from those given. Optional ingredients, variations, or serving suggestions have not been included in the calculations.

Recipes using raw or very lightly cooked eggs should be avoided by infants, the elderly, pregnant women, and people with weakened immune systems. Pregnant and breast-feeding women are advised to avoid eating peanuts and peanut products. People with nut allergies should be aware that some of the prepared ingredients used in the recipes in this book may contain nuts. Always check the packaging before use.

In recipes that call for black coffee or strong black coffee, cafetiere or instant coffee should be used and made up with hot water to taste.

coffee

introduction

Coffee is much more than just a drink to help jump-start your day. This much-loved stimulant is a universal favorite in cooking, and it tastes as good in simple recipes as it does in more complex, luxurious ones. Coffee has an intense, heady aroma and adds a nuttiness and rich, fabulous flavor to whatever you're cooking. Think of coffee as a versatile spice that can be used to season a whole range of delectable recipes, from dinnertime main courses to sweet treats for any time in the day.

This book celebrates the many creative ways that coffee can be used in the kitchen. Chapters cover small cakes and cookies, family cakes, desserts, savory (that is, unsweetened) recipes, and drinks. Here, you'll find an irresistible collection of tried-and-tested coffee recipes, from classic cakes to tasty sweet treats. Coffee can bring out the flavors of meats without imparting an overwhelming taste of coffee. It is also delicious in many drinks and cocktails, although you might want to use decaffeinated later in the evening!

These recipes use all types of coffee: brewed coffee, coffee and chicory essence (available online, or use coffee extract), powder and granules, and coffee-flavored liqueurs. For the best results and maximum indulgence, choose top-quality coffee to create a perfect dish every time. Refrigerate freshly ground coffee in an airtight container and use quickly because it begins to lose flavor after a couple of days. Keep whole roasted beans in an airtight container in a cool, dry place for up to two weeks, or for up to three months in a freezer. You can freeze leftover coffee in ice trays to use at a later date—in iced coffee or stews, for example.

When consumed in moderation, coffee has many health benefits and is full of antioxidants. It may also reduce the risk of developing type-2 diabetes, certain types of cancer, cirrhosis, and gallstones. So now that you know coffee can be a health food, too, there's no excuse not to find plenty of ideas in this book to use and enjoy it, whatever the time of day may be.

small cakes, bars & cookies

mini coffee & maple bundt cakes

ingredients

makes 4

1⅓ cups all-purpose flour,
    plus extra for dusting
1 stick butter, softened,
    plus extra for greasing
½ cup granulated sugar
2 eggs, beaten
2 teaspoons baking powder
1 tablespoon coffee extract or
    flavoring
¼ cup buttermilk

icing

1 cup confectioners' sugar
2 tablespoons maple syrup
1–2 teaspoons water

method

1 Preheat the oven to 350°F. Thoroughly grease four
    1-cup bundt pans, then dust each with a little flour,
    tipping out any excess.

2 Put the butter and sugar into a bowl and beat together
    until pale and creamy. Gradually beat in the eggs.

3 Sift together the flour and baking powder in a separate
    bowl, then fold half the flour into the butter-and-sugar
    mixture. Fold in the coffee and chicory essence and
    buttermilk, followed by the remaining flour.

4 Divide the batter among the prepared pans. Place
    on a baking sheet and bake in the preheated oven for
    25–30 minutes, or until risen and firm to the touch.
    Cool in the pans for 5 minutes, then invert onto a wire
    rack and let cool completely.

5 To make the icing, sift the sugar into a bowl and stir in
    the maple syrup and water and mix until smooth.
    Drizzle the icing over the cakes and let set.

coffee & almond cakes

ingredients

makes 6

1 stick butter, softened,
    plus extra for greasing
1 cup all-purpose flour
1¾ teaspoons baking powder
½ cup firmly packed light
    brown sugar
2 eggs, beaten
¼ cup almond meal
    (ground almonds)
2 teaspoons instant coffee
    granules, dissolved in
    2 tablespoons hot milk
2 tablespoons slivered almonds,
    toasted, to decorate

buttercream
6 tablespoons butter, softened
1⅓ cups confectioners' sugar
2 teaspoons coffee extract or
    flavoring

method

1 Preheat the oven to 350°F. Grease six ¾-cup mini loaf pans and line the bottoms with parchment paper.

2 Sift together the flour and baking powder into a bowl and add the sugar, butter, eggs, and almond meal. Beat with an electric mixer for 2–3 minutes, until smooth and creamy. Beat in the dissolved coffee.

3 Divide the batter among the prepared pans, smoothing the surfaces with a small spatula. Place the pans on a baking sheet and bake the cakes in the preheated oven for 20–25 minutes, or until risen, golden, and just firm to the touch. Let cool in the pans for 5 minutes, then carefully invert onto a wire rack and let cool completely.

4 To make the buttercream, put the butter into a bowl and gradually beat in the sugar, then beat in the coffee and chicory essence until smooth. Spread the buttercream over the cakes and sprinkle with the slivered almonds.

coffee & pecan streusel muffins

ingredients

makes 12

2 cups all-purpose flour
1 tablespoon baking powder
1/2 cup finely chopped pecans
1/2 cup granulated sugar
6 tablespoons butter,
   chilled and coarsely grated
1 extra-large egg, beaten
1/2 cup milk
1/4 cup cold strong black coffee

streusel topping

1/3 cup all-purpose flour
2 tablespoons butter
1/4 cup chopped pecans
1 1/2 teaspoons instant coffee
   granules, finely ground
2 tablespoons raw sugar

method

1 Preheat the oven to 400°F. Line a 12-cup muffin pan with 12 muffin cups.

2 Sift together the flour and baking powder into a large bowl and stir in the nuts and sugar. Add the butter and stir with a fork to coat in the flour mixture.

3 Beat together the egg, milk, and coffee and stir into the dry ingredients. Mix lightly until just combined, being careful to avoid overbeating the mixture. Divide the batter among the muffin cups.

4 To make the topping, put the flour in a bowl and rub in the butter to make fine crumbs. Stir in the nuts, coffee, and sugar. Sprinkle the streusel topping evenly over the muffins.

5 Bake in the preheated oven for 20–25 minutes, or until risen, golden, and just firm to the touch. Cool for 5 minutes, then transfer to a wire rack and let cool completely.

irish coffee muffins

ingredients

makes 12

1 tablespoon sunflower or peanut
    oil, for brushing (if using)
2¼ cups all-purpose flour
1 tablespoon baking powder
pinch of salt
6 tablespoons butter
¼ cup raw sugar
1 extra-large egg, beaten
½ cup heavy cream
1 teaspoon almond extract
2 tablespoons strong coffee
2 tablespoons coffee-flavored
    liqueur
¼ cup Irish whiskey
whipped heavy cream,
    to serve (optional)

method

1 Preheat the oven to 400°F. Brush a 12-cup muffin pan
with sunflower oil, or line it with 12 muffin cups. Sift th
flour, baking powder, and salt into a large mixing bowl

2 In a separate large bowl, cream together the butter
and sugar, then stir in the beaten egg. Pour in the
heavy cream, almond extract, coffee, coffee liqueur,
and whiskey and stir together. Add the whiskey mixtu
to the flour mixture and then gently stir until just
combined. Do not overstir the batter—it is fine for it to
be a little lumpy.

3 Divide the muffin batter evenly among the 12 muffin
cups (they should be about two-thirds full). Bake in
the preheated oven for 20 minutes, or until risen and
golden. Remove the muffins from the oven and serve
warm, or place them on a wire rack to cool. If liked,
slice off the tops and sandwich the muffins with
whipped heavy cream, to serve.

after-dinner coffee liqueur muffins

ingredients

makes 12

oil or melted butter,
   for greasing (if using)
2 tablespoons instant
   coffee granules
2 tablespoons boiling water
2¼ cups all-purpose flour
1 tablespoon baking powder
pinch of salt
½ cup firmly packed light
   brown sugar
2 eggs
½ cup milk
6 tablespoons butter,
   melted and cooled
⅓ cup coffee liqueur
¼ cup raw sugar

method

1 Preheat the oven to 400°F. Grease a 12-cup muffin pan or line with 12 muffin cups. Put the coffee granules and boiling water in a cup and stir until dissolved. Let cool.

2 Meanwhile, sift together the flour, baking powder, and salt into a large bowl. Stir in the brown sugar.

3 Lightly beat the eggs in a large bowl, then beat in the milk, butter, dissolved coffee, and coffee liqueur. Make a well in the center of the dry ingredients and pour in the beaten liquid ingredients. Stir gently until just combined; do not overmix.

4 Spoon the batter into the muffin cups. Sprinkle the raw sugar over the tops of the muffins. Bake in the preheated oven for about 20 minutes, until well risen, golden brown, and firm to the touch.

5 Let the muffins cool in the pan for 5 minutes, then serve warm or transfer to a wire rack and let cool.

marbled coffee muffins

ingredients

makes 12

⅓ cup sunflower oil or
    6 tablespoons butter,
    melted and cooled,
    plus extra for greasing
2¼ cups all-purpose flour
1 tablespoon baking powder
pinch of salt
½ cup granulated sugar
2 eggs
1 cup milk
1 teaspoon vanilla extract
2 tablespoons espresso
    coffee powder

method

1 Preheat the oven to 400°F. Grease a 12-cup muffin pan.
  Sift together the flour, baking powder, and salt into a
  large bowl. Stir in the sugar.

2 Put the eggs in a bowl and beat lightly, then beat in
  the milk, oil, and vanilla extract. Make a well in the
  center of the dry ingredients and pour in the beaten
  liquid ingredients. Stir gently until just combined;
  do not overmix.

3 Divide the batter between two bowls. Sift the coffee
  powder into one bowl and mix together. Using
  teaspoons, spoon the batters into the muffin cups,
  alternating the coffee batter and the plain batter.

4 Bake in the preheated oven for 20 minutes, or until well
  risen, golden brown, and firm to the touch. Let cool in
  the pan for 5 minutes, then serve warm or transfer to a
  wire rack to cool completely.

coffee fudge cupcakes

ingredients

makes 28

1⅓ cups all-purpose flour
1 tablespoon baking powder
1½ sticks unsalted butter, softened
1 cup granulated sugar
3 eggs, beaten
1 teaspoon coffee extract or
    flavoring
2 tablespoons milk
chocolate-covered coffee beans,
    to decorate

frosting

4 tablespoons unsalted butter
½ cup firmly packed light
    brown sugar
2 tablespoons light cream or milk
½ teaspoon coffee extract or
    flavoring
3¼ cups confectioners' sugar, sifted

method

1 Preheat the oven to 375°F. Line three 12-cup muffin pans with 28 muffin cups.

2 Sift the flour and baking powder into a large bowl and add the butter, granulated sugar, eggs, and coffee extract. Beat well until the mixture is smooth, then beat in the milk.

3 Divide the batter among the muffin cups. Bake in the preheated oven for 15–20 minutes, or until risen, firm, and golden brown. Transfer the cupcakes to a wire rack to cool.

4 To make the frosting, place the butter, brown sugar, cream, and coffee extract in a saucepan over medium heat and stir until melted and smooth. Bring to a boil and boil, stirring, for 2 minutes. Remove from the heat and beat in the confectioners' sugar.

5 Stir the frosting until smooth and thick, then spoon into a pastry bag fitted with a large star tip. Pipe a swirl of frosting on top of each cupcake and top with a coffee bean.

feather-iced coffee cupcakes

ingredients

makes 16

1 tablespoon instant
  coffee granules
1 tablespoon boiling water
1 stick butter, softened,
  or soft margarine
½ cup firmly packed light
  brown sugar
2 eggs
¾ cup all-purpose flour
1½ teaspoons baking powder
2 tablespoons sour cream

icing

1¾ cups confectioners' sugar
4 teaspoons warm water
1 teaspoon instant coffee granules
2 teaspoons boiling water

method

1 Preheat the oven to 375°F. Line two 12-cup muffin pans with 16 muffin cups. Put the coffee granules in a small bowl, add the boiling water, and stir until dissolved. Let cool for 5 minutes.

2 Put the butter, sugar, and eggs in a large bowl. Sift in the flour and baking powder and beat until smooth. Add the dissolved coffee and sour cream and beat until mixed. Spoon the batter into the muffin cups.

3 Bake in the preheated oven for 20 minutes, or until well risen and golden. Cool on a wire rack.

4 To make the icing, sift ¾ cup of the confectioners' sugar into a bowl and add enough warm water to mix until thick enough to coat the back of a wooden spoon. Dissolve the coffee in the boiling water. Sift the remaining confectioners' sugar into a bowl and stir in the dissolved coffee. Ice the cakes with the white icing, then pipe the coffee icing in parallel lines on top. Draw a toothpick across the piped lines in both directions to create a feather pattern. Let set before serving.

mocha cherry cupcakes

ingredients

makes 12

3 ounces semisweet chocolate, broken into pieces

1¼ cups all-purpose flour

1¾ teaspoons baking powder

1 tablespoon unsweetened cocoa powder

1½ tablespoons instant coffee powder

2 eggs, lightly beaten

4 tablespoons butter, softened

3 tablespoons milk

½ cup firmly packed light brown sugar

24 fresh cherries, pitted

confectioners' sugar, for dusting

method

1 Preheat the oven to 350°F. Line a 12-cup muffin pan with muffin cups.

2 Put the chocolate in a heatproof bowl, set the bowl over a saucepan of gently simmering water, and heat until melted. Let cool for 5 minutes.

3 Sift the flour, baking powder, and cocoa powder into a bowl and add the coffee powder, eggs, butter, milk, and brown sugar. Beat with an electric mixer for 2–3 minutes, until smooth. Fold in the melted chocolate.

4 Spoon the batter into the muffin cups. Top each cupcake with two cherries. Bake in the preheated oven for 20–25 minutes, or until risen and firm to the touch. Transfer to a wire rack and let cool. Dust with confectioners' sugar before serving.

coffee crumb cakes

ingredients

makes 18

topping

⅔ cup all-purpose flour
5 tablespoons butter,
    cut into pieces
½ teaspoon ground allspice
1½ teaspoons ground
    espresso coffee
⅓ cup granulated sugar
4 tablespoons butter, softened,
    plus extra for greasing
½ cup granulated sugar
1 egg
½ cup sour cream
1 cup all-purpose flour
1½ teaspoons baking powder

icing

⅔ cup confectioners' sugar, sifted
1 tablespoon strong espresso
    coffee, cooled

method

1 Preheat the oven to 350°F. Grease a shallow 8-inch square cake pan and line with parchment paper.

2 To make the topping, put the all-purpose flour, butter, allspice, and coffee in a food processor or blender and process until the mixture starts to resemble coarse bread crumbs. Add the granulated sugar and process again briefly. Transfer the mixture to a mixing bowl.

3 To make the cake, put the butter, granulated sugar, egg, and sour cream in the food processor or blender. Sift in the flour and baking powder, then process until smooth and creamy. Transfer to the pan and smooth level with a spatula. Sprinkle the topping evenly over the top. Bake in the preheated oven for 30–35 minutes or until risen and firm to the touch and a toothpick inserted into the center comes out clean. Let cool in the pan for 10 minutes, then transfer to a wire rack to cool completely.

4 To make the icing, put all but 2 tablespoons of the confectioners' sugar in a small mixing bowl and add the coffee. Beat to a smooth paste that falls in a thick trail from the spoon, adding a little more confectioners' sugar, if necessary. Cut the cake into three even pieces, then cut across to make 18 rectangular pieces. Drizzle with the icing.

mocha raspberry crumb bars

ingredients

makes 8

1½ sticks butter, softened,
    plus extra for greasing
2 cups all-purpose flour, sifted
1½ tablespoons instant
    coffee powder
½ cup granulated sugar
⅓ cup raspberry preserves
⅓ cup chopped mixed nuts
2 tablespoons raw sugar

method

1 Preheat the oven to 350°F. Grease a shallow 8-inch square cake pan and line with parchment paper.

2 Put the butter, flour, instant coffee powder, and granulated sugar into a food processor or blender and process for a few seconds until the mixture starts to clump together.

3 Press three-quarters of the shortbread dough into the bottom of the prepared pan in an even layer. Smooth level with a spatula.

4 Bake in the preheated oven for 20 minutes, or until pale golden. Remove from the oven and let cool for 5 minutes. Spread the preserves over the shortbread layer. Mix the nuts and raw sugar into the remaining shortbread dough and sprinkle it over the preserves, pressing down gently.

5 Return to the oven for an additional 20–25 minutes, or until the topping is golden brown. Let cool completely in the pan, then remove and cut into eight bars.

variation

Replace the raspberry preserves with apricot preserves or blueberry preserves.

cinnamon coffee rolls

ingredients

makes 9

3¼ cups white bread flour,
    plus extra for dusting
¼ teaspoon salt
1½ teaspoons active dry yeast
¼ cup granulated sugar
4 tablespoons butter, melted,
    plus extra for greasing
1 egg, beaten
1 cup lukewarm milk
oil, for greasing
1 cup confectioners' sugar,
    mixed to a smooth icing
    with 1 tablespoon water,
    to decorate

filling

3 tablespoons butter, softened
¼ cup firmly packed dark
    brown sugar
1½ teaspoons instant coffee
    granules, finely ground
1 teaspoon ground cinnamon

method

1 Sift the flour and salt into a large bowl. Stir in the yeast
    and sugar and make a well in the center. Beat together
    the butter, egg, and milk in another bowl, then pour into
    the well and mix to a dough. Turn out the dough onto a
    lightly floured surface and knead for 5–6 minutes, until
    smooth and elastic, adding more flour if it is too sticky.
    Place the dough in a bowl, cover with lightly oiled plastic
    wrap, and let rest in a warm place for 1½ hours, or until
    doubled in size. Grease a 9-inch square cake pan.

2 Turn out the dough onto a floured surface and lightly
    knead for 1 minute. Roll out to a 12-inch square. To
    make the filling, spread the butter over the dough. Mix
    together the sugar, coffee, and cinnamon and sprinkle
    over the butter in an even layer. Roll up the dough from
    one side. Using a sharp knife, cut into nine circles and
    place the rolls, cut-side up, in the prepared pan. Cover
    loosely with oiled plastic wrap and let rest for 40–50
    minutes, or until doubled in size. Meanwhile, preheat
    the oven to 400°F.

3 Bake the rolls in the preheated oven for 18–20 minutes,
    or until risen and golden. Let cool for 10 minutes in the
    pan, then invert onto a wire rack to cool completely.

4 Drizzle the icing over the rolls, let set, then pull
    apart to serve.

coffee caramel éclairs

ingredients

makes 12

choux dough

⅔ cup water
4 tablespoons butter,
    plus extra for greasing
½ cup all-purpose flour, sifted
2 eggs, lightly beaten

filling

1¼ cups heavy cream
¼ cup rum
1 tablespoon confectioners' sugar

coffee caramel

1 cup granulated sugar
½ cup water
1 teaspoon instant coffee

method

1 Put the water and butter in a saucepan and heat gent until the butter melts, then turn up the heat and bring it rapidly to a boil. Immediately add all the flour, remove the pan from the heat, and stir the mixture into a past that leaves the sides of the pan clean.

2 Meanwhile, preheat the oven to 425°F. Grease a baking sheet and prepare a pastry bag fitted with a plain ¾-inch tip. Gradually beat the eggs into the flour past and continue beating until it is smooth and glossy. Spoon the paste into the bag and pipe 12 strips of paste on the baking sheet.

3 Bake for 15 minutes. Reduce the oven temperature to 375°F and cook for an additional 20–25 minutes, until the éclairs are risen, browned, and crisp. Transfer to a wire rack, slitting each pastry lengthwise along the sid to let steam escape. Let cool.

4 Whip the cream with the rum and confectioners' suga Pipe into the pastries and place them close together on the wire rack, putting it over a baking sheet.

5 Put the sugar in a saucepan and add the water. Heat gently until the sugar has dissolved. Bring to a boil and boil rapidly, without stirring, until the syrup turns golde Remove from the heat and stir in the coffee using a metal fork. Drizzle over the éclairs. Let set and cool.

cappuccino squares

ingredients

makes 15

2 sticks butter, softened,
    plus extra for greasing
1¾ cups all-purpose flour
3½ teaspoons baking powder
1 teaspoon unsweetened cocoa
    powder, plus extra for dusting
1 cup granulated sugar
4 eggs, beaten
3 tablespoons instant coffee
    powder, dissolved in
    2 tablespoons hot water

white chocolate frosting

4 ounces white chocolate,
    broken into pieces
4 tablespoons butter, softened
3 tablespoons milk
1⅓ cups confectioners' sugar

method

1 Preheat the oven to 350°F. Lightly grease and line the
    bottom of a shallow 11 x 7-inch cake pan.

2 Sift the flour, baking powder, and cocoa into a bowl
    and add the butter, granulated sugar, eggs, and coffee.
    Beat well, by hand or using an electric mixer, until
    smooth, then spoon the batter into the prepared pan
    and smooth the surface with a spatula.

3 Bake in the preheated oven for 35–40 minutes, or until
    risen and firm to the touch, then invert onto a wire rack
    and let cool completely.

4 To make the frosting, put the chocolate, butter,
    and milk in a heatproof bowl set over a saucepan
    of simmering water and stir until the chocolate has
    melted. Remove the bowl from the pan and sift in the
    confectioners' sugar. Beat until smooth, then spread
    over the cake. Dust the top of the cake with sifted
    cocoa, then cut into squares.

variation

To make a coffee frosting, substitute 2–3 teaspoons
instant coffee for the white chocolate.

coffee madeleines

ingredients

makes 12

3 tablespoons butter, melted,
plus extra for greasing
½ cup all-purpose flour,
plus extra for dusting
1 extra-large egg
¼ cup granulated sugar
1 teaspoon coffee extract or
flavoring
½ teaspoon baking powder

icing

⅔ cup confectioners' sugar, sifted
4–5 teaspoons strong black coffee

method

1 Preheat the oven to 375°F. Grease a 12-cup madeleine pan with butter, then lightly dust with flour, tipping out any excess.

2 Put the egg, sugar, and coffee into a heatproof bowl set over a saucepan of simmering water. Beat with an electric mixer until the mixture is thick and pale and leaves a trail on the surface when the beaters are lifted.

3 Sift the flour and baking powder. Add half the flour mixture to the egg-sugar mixture and fold in gently, then pour over half the butter and fold in until just incorporated. Repeat with the remaining flour mixture and butter.

4 Spoon the batter into the prepared pan, being careful to avoid overfilling the cups. Bake in the preheated oven for 8–10 minutes, or until risen and springy to the touch. Let cool in the pan for 5 minutes, then turn out onto a wire rack and let cool completely.

5 To make the icing, put the sugar and coffee in a small bowl and beat together until smooth. Dip each madeleine in the icing to coat just halfway. Let set on a wire rack.

marbled mocha whoopie pies

ingredients

makes 10

2 cups all-purpose flour
1 teaspoon baking soda
large pinch of salt
1 stick butter, softened
¾ cup granulated sugar
1 extra-large egg, beaten
⅔ cup buttermilk
1 teaspoon vanilla extract
1 teaspoon cold strong black coffee
    or coffee extract
1 tablespoon unsweetened
    cocoa powder

chocolate & cream filling

5 ounces semisweet chocolate,
    finely chopped
2 cups heavy cream
1 tablespoon strong black coffee,
    cooled

method

1 Preheat the oven to 350°F. Line two to three large baking sheets with parchment paper. Sift the all-purpose flour, baking soda, and salt.

2 Put the butter and sugar in a bowl and beat with an electric mixer until pale and fluffy. Beat in the egg, then half the flour mixture, and, finally, the buttermilk. Stir in the rest of the flour, reserving 1 tablespoon. Transfer ha the batter to a second bowl. Stir the vanilla extract and remaining tablespoon of flour mixture into one bowl. St the coffee and cocoa powder into the second bowl. Sv the two batters together to create a marbled effect.

3 Spoon 20 mounds of the batter onto the baking sheets, spaced well apart. Bake in the preheated ove one sheet at a time, for 10–12 minutes, until risen an just firm to the touch. Let cool for 5 minutes, then transfer to a wire rack and let cool completely.

4 Put the chocolate in a heatproof bowl. Heat 1 cup of the cream and the coffee in a saucepan until boiling, then pour over the chocolate and stir until the chocolate has melted. Let cool for 20–30 minutes, stirring occasionally, until thickened. Whip the rest of the cream into firm peaks. Spread the chocolate mixture on the flat side of half of the cakes and top with the whipped cream. Top with the rest of the cak

coffee cream macaroons

ingredients
makes 16

¾ cup almond meal
    (ground almonds)
1 teaspoon coffee granules,
    finely crushed
1 cup confectioners' sugar
2 extra-large egg whites
¼ cup superfine sugar or
    granulated sugar
1 tablespoon amber sugar crystals,
    lightly crushed

filling

½ cup cream cheese
2 tablespoons unsalted
    butter, softened
2 teaspoons strong black
    coffee, cooled
1 cup confectioners' sugar, sifted

method

1 Line two baking sheets with parchment paper. Put the almond meal, coffee granules, and confectioners' sugar in a food processor or blender and process for 15 seconds. Sift the mixture into a bowl.

2 Put the egg whites in a large bowl and beat until they form soft peaks. Gradually beat in the superfine sugar to make a firm, glossy meringue. Using a spatula, fold the almond mixture into the meringue, one-third at a time. Continue to cut and fold the mixture until it forms a shiny batter with a thick, ribbon-like consistency.

3 Pour the mixture into a pastry bag fitted with a ½-inch plain tip. Pipe 32 small circles onto the prepared baking sheets. Tap the baking sheets firmly on a work surface to remove air bubbles. Sprinkle over the sugar crystals. Let stand at room temperature for 30 minutes. Preheat the oven to 325°F.

4 Bake in the preheated oven for 10–15 minutes. Cool for 10 minutes, then carefully peel the macaroons off the parchment paper. Let cool completely.

5 To make the filling, put all the ingredients in a bowl and, using an electric mixer, beat until smooth. Use to sandwich together pairs of macaroons.

coffee cream & walnut cookies

ingredients
makes about 30

2 sticks butter, softened
¾ cup granulated sugar
1 egg yolk, lightly beaten
2 teaspoons vanilla extract
1¾ cups all-purpose flour
pinch of salt
⅔ cup ground walnuts
½ cup finely chopped walnuts

coffee cream
6 tablespoons butter, softened
1¼ cups confectioners' sugar
1½ teaspoons strong black
    coffee, cooled

method

1 Put the butter and sugar in a large bowl and beat together until light and fluffy, then beat in the egg yolk and vanilla extract. Sift the flour and salt into the mixture, add the ground walnuts, and stir until combined. Halve the dough, shape into balls, wrap in plastic wrap, and chill in the refrigerator for 30–60 minutes.

2 Preheat the oven to 375°F. Line two baking sheets with parchment paper. Unwrap the dough and roll out between two sheets of parchment paper. Cut out cookies with a 2½-inch fluted circle cutter and place them on the baking sheets, spaced well apart.

3 Bake in the preheated oven for 10–15 minutes, or until light golden brown. Let cool on the baking sheets for 5–10 minutes, then transfer the cookies to wire racks cool completely.

4 To make the coffee cream, beat the butter and confectioners' sugar in a bowl until smooth and thoroughly combined, then beat in the coffee. Sandwich together the cookies in pairs with the coffee cream, pressing gently so that the cream oozes out of the sides. Smooth the sides with a dampened finger. Spread out the chopped walnuts in a shallow dish and roll the cookies in them to coat the sides of the filling

mocha walnut cookies

ingredients

makes about 16

1 stick butter, softened,
    plus extra for greasing
½ cup firmly packed light
    brown sugar
⅓ cup granulated sugar
1 teaspoon vanilla extract
1 tablespoon instant coffee
    granules, dissolved in
    1 tablespoon hot water
1 egg
1⅓ cups all-purpose flour
½ teaspoon baking powder
¼ teaspoon baking soda
⅓ cup milk chocolate chips
½ cup coarsely chopped walnuts

method

1 Preheat the oven to 350°F and grease two large
baking sheets.

2 Put the butter and sugars in a large bowl and beat
together until light and fluffy. Put the vanilla extract,
coffee, and egg in a separate bowl and beat together.
Gradually add the coffee mixture to the butter and
sugar, beating until fluffy. Sift the flour, baking powder
and baking soda into the mixture and fold in carefully.
Fold in the chocolate chips and walnuts.

3 Spoon heaping teaspoons of the dough onto the
prepared baking sheets, spaced well apart. Bake in the
preheated oven for 10–15 minutes, or until crisp on
the outside but soft inside. Let the cookies cool on the
baking sheets for 2 minutes, then transfer to wire racks
to cool completely.

peanut & coffee cookies

ingredients

makes 14

1 stick butter, softened,
    plus extra for greasing
½ cup firmly packed light
    brown sugar
2 teaspoons coffee extract or
    flavoring
1 teaspoon maple syrup or
    light corn syrup
1⅓ cups all-purpose flour
2 teaspoons baking powder
½ cup coarsely chopped unsalted,
    skinned peanuts

method

1 Preheat the oven to 350°F and grease two large
   baking sheets.

2 Put the butter and sugar in a bowl and beat together
   until pale and creamy. Beat in the coffee and maple
   syrup. Sift in the flour and baking powder, then add
   the peanuts and mix to form a coarse dough.

3 Divide the dough into 14 even balls and place on the
   prepared baking sheets, allowing plenty of room for
   the cookies to spread. Slightly flatten each ball with
   your fingertips.

4 Bake in the preheated oven for 12–14 minutes, or unt
   just set and pale golden. Let cool on the baking sheet
   for 5 minutes, then transfer to a wire rack to cool
   completely. The cookies will become firm as they coo

cappuccino cookies

ingredients

makes about 30

2 envelopes instant cappuccino
1 tablespoon hot water
2 sticks butter, softened
¾ cup granulated sugar
1 egg yolk, lightly beaten
2¼ cups all-purpose flour
pinch of salt

topping

6 ounces white chocolate,
    broken into pieces
unsweetened cocoa powder,
    for dusting

method

1 Put the instant cappuccino into a small bowl and stir in the hot water to make a paste. Put the butter and sugar in a large bowl and beat together until light and fluffy, then beat in the egg yolk and cappuccino paste. Sift together the flour and salt into the mixture and stir until combined. Halve the dough, shape into balls, wrap in plastic wrap, and chill for 30–60 minutes.

2 Preheat the oven to 375°F. Line two large baking sheets with parchment paper. Unwrap the dough and roll it out between two sheets of parchment paper. Cut out cookies with a 2½-inch circle cutter and place them on the prepared baking sheets, spaced well apart. Bake in the preheated oven for 10–12 minutes, or until golden brown. Let cool for 5–10 minutes, then transfer to wire racks to cool completely.

3 Place the wire racks over a sheet of parchment paper. Put the chocolate in a heatproof bowl, set the bowl over a saucepan of gently simmering water, and heat until melted. Let cool, then spoon the chocolate over the cookies. Let the chocolate set, then dust lightly with cocoa powder.

espresso sugar cookies

ingredients

makes 14

1 stick butter, softened,
plus extra for greasing

¼ cup granulated sugar

1 teaspoon espresso coffee powder

1 cup all-purpose flour,
plus extra for dusting

1 tablespoon amber sugar crystals,
lightly crushed

method

1 Put the butter and sugar in a bowl and beat together until pale and fluffy. Beat in the coffee powder. Sift in the flour and mix to a soft dough. Gather together the dough with your hands and knead gently on a lightly floured surface until smooth. Wrap in plastic wrap and chill in the refrigerator for 1 hour.

2 Preheat the oven to 350°F. Grease two baking sheets.

3 Roll out the dough on a lightly floured surface to a thickness of ¼ inch. Use a 2½-inch circle fluted cutter to stamp out 14 circles, rerolling the dough as necessary. Place on the prepared baking sheets. Sprinkle some sugar crystals in the center of each cookie, pressing down gently.

4 Bake in the preheated oven for 10–14 minutes, or until the cookies are light golden around the edges. Let cool for 5 minutes, then transfer to a wire rack and let cool completely.

chocolate & coffee oatmeal cookies

ingredients

makes 24

1½ sticks butter, plus extra
    for greasing
1 cup firmly packed light
    brown sugar
1 egg
½ cup all-purpose flour, plus extra
    for dusting (optional)
1 teaspoon baking soda
pinch of salt
½ cup whole-wheat flour
1 tablespoon wheat bran
1 cup semisweet
    chocolate chips
2 cups rolled oats
1 tablespoon strong coffee
¾ cup hazelnuts, toasted and
    coarsely chopped

method

1 Preheat the oven to 375°F. Grease two large baking
   sheets. Put the butter and sugar in a large bowl
   and beat together until light and fluffy. Add the
   egg and beat well. Sift the all-purpose flour, baking
   soda, and salt into another bowl, then add in the
   whole-wheat flour and bran. Mix in the egg mixture,
   then stir in the chocolate chips, oats, coffee, and
   hazelnuts and mix well.

2 Place 24 heaping tablespoons of the dough on
   the prepared baking sheets, spaced well apart.
   Alternatively, with lightly floured hands, break off
   pieces of the dough and roll into 24 balls, place on
   the baking sheets, then flatten.

3 Bake in the preheated oven for 16–18 minutes, or
   until golden brown. Let cool for 5 minutes, then
   transfer to a wire rack to cool completely.

coffee & hazelnut biscotti

ingredients

makes 20

4 tablespoons unsalted butter,
    plus extra for greasing
½ cup granulated sugar
1 egg, beaten
⅓ cup candied peel
⅓ cup blanched hazelnuts
2 teaspoons espresso
    coffee powder
1⅓ cups all-purpose flour
½ teaspoon baking powder

method

1 Preheat the oven to 350°F. Grease a large baking shee

2 Put the butter and sugar in a large bowl and beat
   together until pale and creamy. Gradually beat in the
   egg, then stir in the candied peel, hazelnuts, and coff

3 Sift in the flour and baking powder and mix to a
   soft dough. Halve the dough and shape each piece
   into an 8 x 4-inch rectangle. Place on the prepared
   baking sheet.

4 Bake in the preheated oven for 20–25 minutes, or un
   just firm. Do not turn off the oven. Let cool on the
   baking sheet for 10 minutes, then, using a spatula,
   transfer each rectangle to a cutting board and cut in
   ten slices.

5 Place the slices, cut-side down, on the baking sheet.
   Return to the oven and bake for another 8–10 minut
   or until golden and crisp. Transfer to a wire rack and l
   cool completely.

family cakes

mocha layer cake

ingredients

serves 8

butter, for greasing
1²/₃ cups all-purpose flour
1 tablespoon baking powder
¹/₄ cup unsweetened
   cocoa powder
¹/₂ cup granulated sugar
2 eggs, beaten
2 tablespoons light corn syrup
²/₃ cup vegetable oil
²/₃ cup milk

filling

1 teaspoon instant coffee
1 tablespoon boiling water
1¹/₄ cups heavy cream
2 tablespoons confectioners' sugar

to decorate

½ cup semisweet chocolate, grated
chocolate curls
confectioners' sugar, for dusting

method

1 Preheat the oven to 350°F. Lightly grease three shallow 7-inch round cake pans. Sift the flour, baking powder, and cocoa into a large bowl, then stir in the sugar. Make a well in the center and stir in the eggs, syrup, oil, and milk. Beat with a wooden spoon, gradually mixing in the dry ingredients to make a smooth batter. Divide the batter among the prepared pans.

2 Bake in the preheated oven for 35–45 minutes, or until springy to the touch. Cool in the pans for 5 minutes, then turn out and cool completely on a wire rack.

3 To make the filling, dissolve the instant coffee in the boiling water and put in a large bowl with the cream and confectioners' sugar. Whip until the cream is just holding its shape, then use half the cream to sandwich together the three cakes. Spread the remaining cream over the top and sides of the cake. Press the grated chocolate into the cream around the side of the cake.

4 Transfer the cake to a serving plate. Lay the chocolate curls over the top of the cake. Cut a few thin strips of parchment paper and place on top of the chocolate curls. Dust lightly with confectioners' sugar to create a striped pattern, then carefully remove the paper. Serve.

coffee & walnut ring

ingredients

serves 10

oil or melted butter,
    for greasing
1⅓ cups all-purpose flour
1 tablespoon baking powder
1½ sticks unsalted butter, softened
¾ cup firmly packed light
    brown sugar
3 eggs, beaten
1 teaspoon coffee extract
½ cup walnut pieces, chopped,
    plus extra walnut halves
    to decorate
¼ cup maple syrup

method

1 Preheat the oven to 325°F. Grease a 1½-quart tube pan, preferably with a nonstick finish.

2 Sift the flour and baking powder into a large bowl and add the butter, sugar, eggs, and coffee. Beat well until the batter is smooth, then stir in the chopped walnuts.

3 Spoon the batter into the prepared pan and smooth the surface with a spatula. Bake in the preheated oven for 40–45 minutes, or until the cake is risen, firm, and golden brown.

4 Let cool in the pan for 10 minutes, then turn out carefully onto a wire rack. While the cake is still warm, spoon half the maple syrup over it. Let cool completely. To serve, top with walnut halves and drizzle with the remaining maple syrup.

gingerbread latte cake

ingredients

serves 10

1½ sticks butter, plus extra
    for greasing
¾ cup firmly packed light
    brown sugar
½ cup light corn syrup
⅓ cup molasses
2 teaspoons instant coffee granules
2¾ cups all-purpose flour
4 teaspoons baking powder
2 teaspoons ground ginger
2 extra-large eggs, beaten

frosting

1 stick butter, softened
3 tablespoons heavy cream
2 teaspoons coffee extract or
    flavoring
1¾ cups confectioners' sugar, sifted
1 tablespoon raw sugar
1 teaspoon instant coffee granules,
    finely ground

method

1 Preheat the oven to 325°F. Grease an 8-inch square cake pan and line with parchment paper.

2 Put the butter, sugar, corn syrup, molasses, and coffee granules in a small saucepan and heat gently until the butter has melted and the sugar has dissolved. Let co for 10 minutes.

3 Sift the flour, baking powder, and ginger into a large bowl. Stir in the melted mixture and the eggs and be until smooth and creamy. Spoon the batter into the pan and smooth the surface with a spatula.

4 Bake the cake in the preheated oven for 1 hour–1 hour 10 minutes, until it is risen, golden brown, and a toothpick inserted into the center comes out clean. Let cool in the pan for 10 minutes, then turn ou onto a wire rack to cool completely.

5 To make the frosting, put the butter into a bowl and beat with an electric mixer for 2–3 minutes, until pale and creamy. Beat in the cream and coffee extract, the gradually beat in the confectioners' sugar and continu to beat for 2–3 minutes, until light and fluffy.

6 Swirl the frosting over the top of the cake. Mix the raw sugar and ground coffee and sprinkle it over the frosting.

pecan coffee layer cake

ingredients

serves 10–12

2½ sticks butter, softened,
  plus extra for greasing
2¼ cups all-purpose flour
1 tablespoon baking powder
1⅓ cups granulated sugar
5 eggs, beaten
1 tablespoon instant coffee
  granules, dissolved in
  2 tablespoons hot water
¾ cup pecans, finely ground
chopped pecans, to decorate

frosting

2 cups cream cheese
2 tablespoons maple syrup
1 cup confectioners' sugar

method

1 Preheat the oven to 350°F. Grease three 9-inch round cake pans and line the bottoms with parchment pape

2 Sift the flour and baking powder into a large bowl. Add the butter, sugar, eggs, and coffee and beat with an electric mixer for 1–2 minutes, until creamy. Fold i the nuts.

3 Divide the batter among the prepared pans and smooth the surfaces with a spatula. Bake in the preheated oven for 20–25 minutes, until risen, golde and just firm to the touch. Let the cakes cool in the pans for 10 minutes, then turn out onto a wire rack t cool completely.

4 To make the frosting, put the cheese and maple syru into a bowl and beat together until blended. Sift in th sugar and beat until smooth.

5 Sandwich together the cakes with one-third of the frosting. Spread the remainder over the top and sides of the cake and decorate with chopped pecans.

coffee & walnut cake

ingredients

serves 8

1½ sticks unsalted butter, softened, plus extra for greasing
¾ cup firmly packed light brown sugar
3 extra-large eggs, beaten
3 tablespoons strong black coffee, - cooled
1⅓ cups all-purpose flour
3½ teaspoons baking powder
1 cup walnut pieces
walnut halves, to decorate

frosting

1 stick unsalted butter, softened
1⅔ cups confectioners' sugar
1 tablespoon strong black coffee, cooled
½ teaspoon vanilla extract

method

1 Preheat the oven to 350°F. Grease two 8-inch round cake pans and line with parchment paper.

2 Beat together the butter and brown sugar until pale and creamy. Gradually add the eggs, beating well aft each addition. Beat in the coffee.

3 Sift the flour and baking powder into the mixture, th fold in lightly and evenly with a metal spoon. Fold in the walnut pieces. Divide the batter between the prepared cake pans and smooth the surfaces with a spatula. Bake in the preheated oven for 20–25 minu or until golden brown and springy to the touch. Inve onto a wire rack to cool completely.

4 To make the frosting, beat together the butter, confectioners' sugar, coffee, and vanilla extract, mixing until smooth and creamy.

5 Use about half the frosting to sandwich together the cakes, then spread the remaining frosting on top of the cake and swirl with a spatula. Decorate with walnut halves.

coffee bundt cake

ingredients

serves 14

2½ sticks butter, softened, plus extra for greasing

3¼ cups all-purpose flour, plus extra for dusting

1 tablespoon baking powder

1 teaspoon baking soda

3 tablespoons espresso coffee powder

½ cup firmly packed light brown sugar

1 cup maple syrup

3 eggs, beaten

1 cup buttermilk

1 cup heavy cream

to decorate

¼ cup maple syrup

1⅔ cups confectioners' sugar

1 tablespoon unsalted butter, melted

1½–2 teaspoons water

20 white and dark chocolate-coated coffee beans

method

1 Preheat the oven to 350°F. Grease and lightly flour a 12-cup (standard size) bundt cake pan. Sift the flour, baking powder, baking soda, and coffee powder into a bowl. In a separate bowl, beat together the butter and sugar until pale and creamy. Gradually beat in the maple syrup. Beat in the eggs slowly, adding 3 tablespoons of the flour mixture to prevent the mixture from curdling.

2 Mix the buttermilk and cream and add half to the butter mixture. Sprinkle in half of the flour mixture and fold gently together. Add the remaining buttermilk and flour mixture and mix until just combined.

3 Spoon the batter into the prepared pan and smooth the surface. Bake in the preheated oven for about 50 minutes, or until well risen and a toothpick inserted into the center comes out clean. Let cool in the pan 10 minutes, then loosen with a knife and turn out on a wire rack to cool completely.

4 Beat the maple syrup in a bowl with 1¼ cups of the confectioners' sugar and the butter until smooth. Transfer the cake to a serving plate and spoon the icing around the top of the cake so that it runs down the sides. Beat the remaining sugar with the water in a bowl to make a smooth paste. Drizzle the icing over the cake and top with the coffee beans.

coffee fruitcake

ingredients

serves 10

1¾ cups mixed dried fruit

⅔ cup firmly packed light brown sugar

1¼ sticks butter, plus extra for greasing

1 cup strong black coffee

2¼ cups all-purpose flour

1 tablespoon baking powder

2 teaspoons allspice

1 extra-large egg, beaten

butter, to serve (optional)

method

1 Put the dried fruit, sugar, butter, and coffee in a large saucepan and heat gently, stirring occasionally, until the butter has melted and the sugar has dissolve Remove from the heat and let cool for 30 minutes.

2 Preheat the oven to 350°F. Grease a 9-inch loaf pan a line the bottom and the two short sides with a strip o parchment paper.

3 Sift the flour, baking powder, and allspice into a large bowl. Make a well in the center and pour in the fruit and coffee mixture and the beaten egg. Stir until thoroughly mixed.

4 Spoon the cake batter into the prepared pan and smooth the surface. Bake in the preheated oven for 1 hour 15 minutes (covering loosely with aluminum f after 50 minutes), or until the cake is firm to the touc and a toothpick inserted into the center comes out clean. Let cool in the pan for 10 minutes, then turn o onto a wire rack to cool completely. Serve sliced, spread with butter, if desired.

mocha stollen

ingredients

serves 10

¾ cup milk

4 tablespoons butter

2 teaspoons instant coffee granules

2¼ cups white bread flour,
plus extra for dusting

2 tablespoons packed light
brown sugar

2 teaspoons active dry yeast

2 teaspoons allspice

¼ teaspoon salt

⅓ cup dried sweetened cranberries

¼ cup golden raisins

2 tablespoons candied peel

1 egg, beaten

vegetable oil, for greasing

6 ounces marzipan, rolled into
a 9-inch log shape

confectioners' sugar, to dust

icing

½ cup confectioners' sugar

2 tablespoons unsweetened
cocoa powder

1½–2 tablespoons milk

method

1 Put the milk, butter, and coffee granules in a small saucepan and heat gently until the butter has melted. Let cool for 10 minutes.

2 Sift the flour into a large bowl and stir in the sugar, yeast, allspice, salt, cranberries, golden raisins, and candied peel. Make a well in the center and stir in the milk mixture and egg. Mix to a soft dough, then turn out onto a lightly floured surface and knead for 5–6 minutes until smooth. Put in a bowl, cover with lightly oiled plastic wrap, and let rest in a warm place for 1½ hours, or until doubled in size. Grease a large baking sheet.

3 Turn out the dough onto a lightly floured surface and lightly knead for 1 minute. Roll out to a 12-inch-long oval. Lay the marzipan down the middle of the dough and fold over the sides to enclose it. Place the stollen, seam-side down, on the prepared baking sheet. Cover with oiled plastic wrap and let rest in a warm place for 40–50 minutes, until doubled in size.

4 Meanwhile, preheat the oven to 375°F. Bake the stollen in the preheated oven for 40–45 minutes, or until golden. Transfer to a wire rack and let cool. Sift the sugar and cocoa powder into a bowl and stir in the milk. Drizzle the icing over the stollen and let set, then dust with confectioners' sugar.

raisin & cinnamon coffee crumb cake

ingredients

serves 10

1½ sticks butter, softened,
   plus extra for greasing
1 cup granulated sugar
3 extra-large eggs, beaten
3 tablespoons strong
   black coffee, cooled
1¼ cups all-purpose flour
2½ teaspoons baking powder
2 teaspoons ground cinnamon
1¼ cups raisins
1 Granny Smith apple, peeled,
   cored, and finely chopped

crumb topping

⅔ cup all-purpose flour
1 teaspoon baking powder
4 tablespoons butter,
   chilled and diced
¼ cup raw sugar
2 teaspoons instant coffee
   granules, finely ground
½ cup chopped mixed nuts
confectioners' sugar, for dusting

method

1 Preheat the oven to 350°F. Grease an 8-inch round springform cake pan and line the bottom with parchment paper.

2 Put the butter and sugar in a large bowl and beat ur pale and fluffy, then gradually beat in the eggs and coffee. Sift the flour, baking powder, and cinnamon over the butter-egg mixture, and fold in gently until thoroughly incorporated, then fold in the raisins. Sp the batter into the prepared pan and sprinkle with t chopped apple.

3 To make the topping, sift the flour and baking powd into a bowl, then add the butter and rub in to make fine crumbs. Stir in the raw sugar, coffee, and nuts. Sprinkle the mixture evenly over the apple.

4 Bake in the preheated oven for 1–1¼ hours, until golden brown, firm to the touch, and a toothpick inserted into the center comes out clean—cover loosely with aluminum foil after about 50 minutes if the crumb topping starts to overbrown. Let cool in the pan for 20 minutes, then unclip the pan and transfer the cake to a wire rack to cool completely. Lightly dust with confectioners' sugar to serve.

banana mocha cake

ingredients

serves 10

1 tablespoon instant
coffee granules

2 tablespoons water

1 cup firmly packed light
brown sugar

1¾ sticks butter, softened,
plus extra for greasing

2¼ cups all-purpose flour,
plus extra for dusting

3 extra-large eggs, beaten

2 small bananas, peeled
and mashed

2½ teaspoons baking powder

frosting

3 ounces semisweet chocolate,
broken into pieces

1 tablespoon unsalted butter

1 tablespoon strong black coffee

method

1 Put the coffee, water, and 2 tablespoons of the sugar
in a small saucepan and heat gently, stirring, until
the coffee and sugar have dissolved. Simmer for
1–2 minutes, until syrupy, then let cool.

2 Preheat the oven to 325°F. Grease and lightly flour a
2½-quart tube cake pan.

3 Put the butter and remaining sugar in a large bowl
beat together until pale and fluffy. Gradually beat in
the eggs, then the coffee syrup. Stir in the mashed
banana, then sift in the flour and baking powder an
fold in thoroughly.

4 Spoon the batter into the prepared pan and smooth
the surface with a spatula. Bake in the preheated ov
for 45–50 minutes, or until the cake is firm, golden, a
a toothpick inserted into the center comes out clea
Let cool in the pan for 10 minutes, then turn out ont
wire rack to cool completely.

5 To make the frosting, put the chocolate, butter, and
coffee in a heatproof bowl set over a saucepan of
simmering water and heat until melted. Remove fro
the heat and stir until smooth. Spoon the frosting
over the top of the cake, gently easing it halfway
down the sides. Let set.

espresso sheet cake

ingredients

serves 12

1½ sticks butter, softened,
    plus extra for greasing
3 tablespoons unsweetened
    cocoa powder
1 tablespoon espresso
    coffee powder
¼ cup boiling water
1⅔ cups all-purpose flour
3½ teaspoons baking powder
1 cup granulated sugar
3 eggs
1 teaspoon vanilla extract
1 tablespoon milk

frosting

1 cup mascarpone cheese
¼ cup granulated sugar
1 tablespoon espresso
    coffee, cooled
¼ cup heavy cream
3 ounces semisweet
    chocolate, melted

method

1 Preheat the oven to 350°F. Grease a 7 x 11-inch sheet
    cake pan and line the bottom with parchment paper.

2 Put the cocoa powder, coffee powder, and boiling
    water in a heatproof bowl and mix together to a
    smooth paste. Let cool for 10 minutes.

3 Sift the flour and baking powder into a bowl and add
    the butter, sugar, eggs, vanilla extract, milk, and cocoa
    mixture. Beat with an electric mixer for 2–3 minutes,
    until smooth and creamy.

4 Spoon the cake batter into the prepared pan and
    smooth the surface with a spatula. Bake in the
    preheated oven for 30–35 minutes, or until risen
    and just firm to the touch. Let the cake cool in
    the pan for 10 minutes, then turn out onto a wire
    rack to cool completely.

5 To make the frosting, put the mascarpone cheese,
    sugar, coffee, and cream in a bowl and beat together
    until smooth. Spread over the top of the cake. Spoon
    the melted chocolate into a paper pastry bag, snip
    off the end, and pipe thin zigzag lines across the
    frosting. Let set.

marble cake

ingredients

serves 10

2 sticks butter, softened,
    plus extra for greasing
2 ounces semisweet chocolate,
    broken into pieces
1 tablespoon strong black coffee
2¼ cups all-purpose flour
4 teaspoons baking powder
1 cup granulated sugar
4 eggs, beaten
½ cup almond meal
    (ground almonds)
2 tablespoons milk
1 teaspoon vanilla extract

icing

4 ounces semisweet chocolate,
    broken into pieces
2 tablespoons butter
2 tablespoons water

method

1 Preheat the oven to 350°F and grease a 1¾-quart tub
cake pan.

2 Put the chocolate and coffee in a heatproof bowl, se
the bowl over a saucepan of gently simmering wate
and heat until melted. Let cool.

3 Sift the flour and baking powder into a bowl. Add th
butter, sugar, eggs, almond meal, and milk. Beat well
until smooth.

4 Transfer half of the batter to a separate bowl and stir
the vanilla extract. Stir the cooled chocolate mixture
into the other half of the batter. Place spoonfuls of th
two batters alternately into the prepared cake pan,
then drag a toothpick through to create a marbled
effect. Smooth the surface with a spatula.

5 Bake in the preheated oven for 50–60 minutes, until
risen and a toothpick inserted into the cake comes c
clean. Let cool in the pan for 5 minutes, then turn ou
onto a wire rack to cool completely.

6 To make the icing, put the chocolate, butter, and wa
in a heatproof bowl, set the bowl over a saucepan of
gently simmering water and heat until melted. Stir a
pour over the top of the cake, working quickly to coa
the top and sides. Let set before serving.

spiced coffee & orange swirl cake

ingredients

serves 8–10

1½ sticks butter, softened,
   plus extra for greasing
⅓ cup pecans
¼ cup firmly packed light
   brown sugar
2 teaspoons allspice
1 tablespoon instant coffee powder
1¾ cups all-purpose flour
3½ teaspoons baking powder
1 cup granulated sugar
3 extra-large eggs, beaten
finely grated rind and juice
   of 1 orange

method

1 Preheat the oven to 350°F. Grease an 8-inch round cake pan and line with parchment paper.

2 Put the nuts, brown sugar, allspice, and coffee powder in a food processor or blender and process for a few seconds until finely ground.

3 Sift the flour and baking powder into a large bowl. Add the butter, granulated sugar, eggs, and orange rind and juice and beat with an electric mixer for 1–2 minutes until smooth and creamy.

4 Spread one-third of the cake batter in the bottom of the prepared pan. Sprinkle over half the nut mixture. Repeat the layers once, then gently spread the remaining cake batter on top. Drag a thin knife through the batter to create a swirled effect.

5 Bake in the preheated oven for 55–65 minutes, or until risen and firm to the touch and a toothpick inserted into the center comes out clean. Let cool in the pan for 10 minutes, then turn out onto a wire rack to cool completely.

mocha-glazed pound cake

ingredients

serves 9

2¼ sticks butter, softened,
    plus extra for greasing
2⅓ cups all-purpose flour
1 teaspoon baking powder
1 cup granulated sugar
1 tablespoon coffee extract
    or flavoring
6 eggs

mocha glaze

4 ounces semisweet chocolate,
    finely chopped
1 tablespoon coffee extract
    or flavoring
1 tablespoon unsalted butter
⅔ cup heavy cream

method

1 Preheat the oven to 350°F. Grease an 8-inch square cake pan and line with parchment paper. Sift the flour and baking powder into a bowl and set aside.

2 Put the butter and sugar in a large bowl and beat with an electric mixer until pale and creamy. Beat in the coffee extract, then beat in the eggs, one at a time, adding a spoonful of the flour mixture after each egg. Fold in the remaining flour. Spoon the batter into the prepared pan and smooth the surface with a spatula.

3 Bake in the preheated oven for 50 minutes–1 hour, or until risen, golden brown, and a toothpick inserted into the center comes out clean. Let cool in the pan for 10 minutes, then turn out the cake onto a wire rack to cool completely.

4 To make the glaze, put the chocolate, coffee extract, and butter in a heatproof bowl. Heat the cream until almost boiling, then pour into the bowl. Stir continuously until the chocolate has melted. Let cool and thicken for about 20 minutes, stirring occasionally. Pour the thick glaze over the cake, allowing it to spill down the sides. Let set before serving.

coffee & walnut swirl

ingredients

serves 6–8

butter, for greasing
3 eggs
1 egg white
½ cup granulated sugar, plus extra
    for sprinkling
1 teaspoon coffee extract
½ cup all-purpose flour, sifted
⅓ cup finely chopped walnuts,
    plus extra to decorate

filling

¾ cup heavy cream
¼ cup confectioners' sugar, plus
    extra for dusting
1 tablespoon coffee liqueur

method

1 Preheat the oven to 400°F. Grease a 13 x 9-inch jelly ro
   pan with butter and line with parchment paper.

2 Put the eggs, egg white, and sugar in a heatproof bo
   over a saucepan of hot water. Beat with an electric
   mixer until pale and thick enough to leave a trail.

3 Beat in the coffee extract, then lightly fold in the flou
   and the finely chopped walnuts with a metal spoon.
   Spoon the batter into the prepared pan, spreading
   evenly. Bake in the preheated oven for 12–15 minute
   until golden brown and firm.

4 Sprinkle a sheet of parchment paper with sugar. Turr
   out the cake onto the sugar-dusted paper and peel o
   the parchment paper from the cooked cake. Trim the
   edges. Quickly roll up the cake from one short side,
   with the paper inside. Let stand on a wire rack to
   cool completely.

5 To make the filling, put the cream, sugar, and liqueur
   in a bowl and beat until the mixture begins to hold
   its shape.

6 Carefully unroll the cake, remove the paper, and spre
   the cream filling over the cake. Roll up carefully. Serv
   the roll dusted with confectioners' sugar and decora
   with coarsely chopped walnuts.

chocolate cake with coffee syrup

ingredients

serves 12

1 stick unsalted butter,
    plus extra for greasing
8 ounces semisweet chocolate,
    broken into pieces
1 tablespoon strong black coffee
4 extra-large eggs
2 egg yolks
½ cup granulated sugar
½ cup all-purpose flour
2 teaspoons ground cinnamon
½ cup almond meal
    (ground almonds)
chocolate-covered coffee beans,
    to decorate

syrup

1¼ cups strong black coffee
½ cup granulated sugar
1 cinnamon stick

method

1 Preheat the oven to 375°F. Grease an 8-inch round ca
pan and line the bottom with parchment paper. Put
the chocolate, butter, and coffee in a heatproof bowl
set the bowl over a saucepan of gently simmering
water, and heat until melted. Stir to blend, then remo
from the heat and cool slightly.

2 Put the whole eggs, egg yolks, and sugar in a separat
bowl and beat together until thick and pale. Sift the
flour and cinnamon over the egg mixture. Add the
almonds and the chocolate mixture and fold in
carefully. Spoon the batter into the prepared pan and
bake in the preheated oven for 35 minutes, or until a
toothpick inserted into the center comes out clean.
Cool slightly before turning out onto a serving plate.

3 Meanwhile, make the syrup. Put the coffee, sugar, an
cinnamon stick in a heavy saucepan and heat gently
stirring, until the sugar has dissolved. Increase the he
and boil for 5 minutes, or until reduced and thickene
slightly. Keep warm. Pierce the surface of the cake wi
a toothpick, then drizzle half the coffee syrup over
the cake. Decorate with chocolate-covered coffee
beans and serve, cut into wedges, with the remainin
coffee syrup.

coffee streusel cake

ingredients

serves 8

1 stick butter, melted and cooled,
    plus extra for greasing
2¼ cups all-purpose flour
1 tablespoon baking powder
⅓ cup granulated sugar
⅔ cup milk
2 eggs
2 tablespoons instant coffee,
    mixed with 1 tablespoon
    boiling water
½ cup chopped almonds
confectioners' sugar, for dusting

topping

⅔ cup all-purpose flour
1 teaspoon baking powder
⅓ cup raw sugar
2 tablespoons butter, diced
1 teaspoon allspice
1 tablespoon water

method

1 Preheat the oven to 375°F. Grease a 9-inch, round springform cake pan and line with parchment paper.

2 Sift the flour and baking powder into a large mixing bowl, then stir in the granulated sugar. In a separate bowl, beat the milk, eggs, melted butter, and coffee mixture and pour onto the dry ingredients. Add the chopped almonds and mix lightly. Spoon the batter into the prepared pan.

3 To make the topping, mix the flour, baking powder, and raw brown sugar. Rub in the butter with your fingertips until the mixture resembles bread crumbs. Sprinkle in the allspice and water and bring the mixture together into loose crumbs. Sprinkle the topping evenly over the surface of the cake batter in the pan.

4 Bake in the preheated oven for about 1 hour, or until a toothpick inserted into the center comes out clean. If the topping starts to brown too quickly, cover loosely with aluminum foil. Let cool in the pan. Turn out, dust with confectioners' sugar, and serve.

sachertorte

ingredients

serves 10

1¼ sticks unsalted butter,
    plus extra for greasing
6 ounces semisweet chocolate,
    broken into pieces
¾ cup granulated sugar
6 eggs, separated
1⅓ cups all-purpose flour

icing

8 ounces semisweet chocolate,
    broken into pieces
5 tablespoons strong black coffee
1⅓ cups confectioners' sugar
⅓ cup apricot preserves, warmed

method

1 Preheat the oven to 300°F. Grease and line a 9-inch round springform cake pan.

2 Put the chocolate in a heatproof bowl, set the bowl over a saucepan of gently simmering water, and hea until melted. In a separate bowl, beat the butter and ⅓ cup of the sugar until pale and fluffy. Add the egg yolks and beat well. Add the chocolate in a thin strea beating well. Sift in the flour and fold it into the mixture. In a separate bowl, beat the egg whites unt they stand in soft peaks. Add the remaining sugar ar beat until glossy. Fold half the egg-white mixture int the chocolate mixture, then fold in the remainder.

3 Spoon into the prepared pan and smooth the top. Bake in the preheated oven for 1–1¼ hours, until a toothpick inserted into the center comes out clean. Cool in the pan for 5 minutes, then transfer to a wire rack to cool completely.

4 To make the icing, melt three-quarters of the chocola and beat in the coffee until smooth. Sift in the sugar and beat. Halve the cake. Spread the preserves over t cut surfaces and sandwich together. Turn out the cak on a wire rack. Spoon the icing over the cake and spread to coat the top and sides. Let set for 5 minutes Transfer to a serving plate and let set for at least 2 hou

chocolate truffle torte

ingredients

serves 10

butter, for greasing
¼ cup granulated sugar
2 eggs
2 tablespoons all-purpose flour
¼ cup unsweetened cocoa powder,
    plus extra to decorate
¼ cup strong black coffee, cooled
2 tablespoons brandy

topping

2½ cups heavy whipping cream
16 ounces semisweet chocolate,
    melted and cooled
confectioners' sugar, to decorate

method

1 Preheat the oven to 425°F. Grease a 9-inch springform cake pan and line the bottom with parchment paper. Place the sugar and eggs in a heatproof bowl and set over a saucepan of hot water. Beat together until pale and mousse-like. Sift the flour and cocoa powder into a separate bowl, then fold gently into the cake batter. Pour into the prepared pan and bake in the preheated oven for 7–10 minutes, or until risen and firm to the touch.

2 Transfer to a wire rack to cool. Wash and dry the pan and replace the cooled cake in the pan. Mix the coffee and brandy and brush over the cake.

3 To make the topping, put the cream in a bowl and whip until soft peaks form. Carefully fold in the cooled chocolate. Pour the chocolate mixture over the cake and chill in the refrigerator for 4–5 hours, or until set.

4 To decorate the torte, sift cocoa powder over the top and remove carefully from the pan. Using strips of cardboard or wax paper as a mask, sift bands of confectioners' sugar over the torte to create a striped pattern. To serve, cut into slices with a hot knife.

white chocolate coffee cake

ingredients

serves 8–10

3 tablespoons unsalted butter,
plus extra for greasing
3 ounces white chocolate, broken
into pieces
²/₃ cup granulated sugar
4 extra-large eggs, beaten
2 tablespoons strong black coffee
1 teaspoon vanilla extract
1 cup all-purpose flour
white chocolate curls,
to decorate

frosting

6 ounces white chocolate, broken
into pieces
6 tablespoons unsalted butter
½ cup crème fraîche or
cream cheese
1 cup confectioners' sugar, sifted
1 tablespoon coffee liqueur or
strong black coffee

method

1 Preheat the oven to 350°F. Grease two 8-inch cake p
and line the bottoms with parchment paper.

2 Put the butter and chocolate in a heatproof bowl se
over a saucepan of hot water and heat on low heat
until just melted. Stir, then remove from the heat.

3 Put the granulated sugar, eggs, coffee, and vanilla
extract in a large heatproof bowl set over a saucepa
of hot water and beat with an electric mixer until th
mixture is pale and thick. Remove from the heat, sif
in the flour, and fold in lightly. Fold in the butter and
chocolate mixture, then divide the batter between
the prepared pans. Bake in the preheated oven for
25–30 minutes, until golden brown and springy
to the touch. Let cool slightly, then turn out onto a
wire rack to cool.

4 To make the frosting, put the chocolate and butter in
heatproof bowl set over a saucepan of hot water and
heat gently until melted. Remove from the heat and
in the crème fraîche, confectioners' sugar, and coffee
liqueur. Chill, stirring occasionally, until the mixture is
thick and glossy. Sandwich the cakes together with
some of the frosting and spread the remainder over t
top and sides, swirling with a spatula. Arrange the wh
chocolate curls over the top and let set.

italian coffee cake

ingredients

serves 8

3 tablespoons butter, melted and
    cooled, plus extra for greasing
4 extra-large eggs
½ cup granulated sugar
1 cup all-purpose flour
unsweetened cocoa powder,
    for dusting
2 ounces semisweet dark
    chocolate, finely grated

espresso syrup

½ cup espresso coffee
½ cup confectioners' sugar

frosting

1 cup mascarpone cheese
⅓ cup granulated sugar
2 tablespoons Marsala wine

method

1 Preheat the oven to 350°F. Grease two 8-inch round
    cake pans and line the bottom with parchment pap

2 Put the eggs and sugar into a heatproof bowl set ov
    a saucepan of simmering water. Beat with an electri
    mixer until the mixture is thick and pale and leaves a
    trail on the surface when the beaters are lifted. Sift i
    the flour and fold in gently. Pour the butter over the
    mixture in a thin stream and fold in until incorporate

3 Divide the batter between the prepared pans and b
    in the preheated oven for 20–25 minutes, until light
    golden and springy to the touch. Let cool in the par
    for 5 minutes, then invert onto a wire rack.

4 To make the syrup, put the coffee and sugar in a sm
    saucepan and bring to a boil. Simmer for 3–4 minut
    until syrupy. Let cool for 10 minutes. Pierce the tops
    the warm cakes all over with a toothpick and spoon
    over the coffee syrup. Let cool completely.

5 To make the frosting, put all the ingredients into a
    bowl and beat together until smooth. Spread half th
    frosting over one cake and sprinkle with half the gra
    chocolate. Top with the second cake and swirl the
    remaining frosting over the top. Dust with the cocoa
    powder and sprinkle with the chocolate.

mocha cake

ingredients

serves 12

2 sticks butter, softened,
plus extra for greasing
1¾ cups self-rising flour
3½ teaspoons baking powder
2 tablespoons unsweetened
cocoa powder
1 cup firmly packed light
brown sugar
4 extra-large eggs, beaten
4 ounces semisweet chocolate,
melted
2 tablespoons granulated sugar
3 tablespoons strong black coffee

frosting

6 tablespoons unsalted
butter, softened
1 cup mascarpone cheese
½ cup confectioners' sugar
2 tablespoons strong black
coffee, cooled
unsweetened cocoa powder,
for dusting
chocolate-coated coffee beans,
to decorate

method

1 Preheat the oven to 350°F. Grease two 8-inch cake pa
and line the bottom with parchment paper.

2 Sift the flour, baking powder, and cocoa powder into
large bowl. Add the butter, brown sugar, and eggs an
using an electric mixer, beat together
for 3–4 minutes, or until the mixture is smooth and
creamy. Fold in the melted chocolate.

3 Divide the batter between the prepared cake pans a
bake in the preheated oven for 25–30 minutes, or un
risen and firm to the touch.

4 Put the granulated sugar and black coffee in a small
saucepan and heat gently for 1–2 minutes. Let cool f
10 minutes. Pierce the tops of the warm cakes all ove
with a toothpick and spoon the coffee syrup over the
cakes. Let the cakes cool completely in the pans.

5 To make the frosting, put the butter and mascarpone
cheese in a bowl and beat together until well blende
Beat in the confectioners' sugar and coffee until smoot

6 Remove the cakes from the pans and sandwich
together with half the frosting. Swirl the remaining
frosting over the top of the cake. Dust with cocoa
powder and decorate with chocolate-coated
coffee beans.

coffee & amaretto cream cake

ingredients

serves 8

1½ sticks butter, softened,
    plus extra for greasing
1⅓ cups all-purpose flour
1 tablespoon baking powder
¾ cup firmly packed light
    brown sugar
3 eggs, beaten
3 tablespoons strong black
    coffee, cooled
2 ounces semisweet chocolate,
    melted, and
    1 tablespoon toasted slivered
    almonds, to decorate

filling

2 cups heavy cream
2–3 tablespoons amaretto

method

1 Preheat the oven to 350°F. Grease two 8-inch round
  cake pans and line the bottom with parchment paper.

2 Sift the flour and baking powder into a bowl and add
  the butter, sugar, eggs, and coffee. Beat with an electric
  mixer for 1–2 minutes, until smooth and creamy. Divide
  the batter between the prepared pans and smooth the
  surface with a spatula.

3 Bake in the preheated oven for 25–30 minutes, or until
  golden brown and springy to the touch. Let cool in the
  pans for 5 minutes, then turn out the cakes onto a wire
  rack to cool completely.

4 To make the filling, put the cream into a bowl with the
  amaretto and whip until it holds soft peaks. Sandwich
  the cakes together with half the cream and spread the
  remainder over the top. Spoon the melted chocolate
  into a paper pastry bag and snip off the end. Pipe swirls
  of chocolate on the top of the cake and sprinkle with
  the slivered almonds.

desserts & other treats

coffee ice cream

ingredients

serves 6

1 ounce semisweet chocolate, plus
    extra to decorate
1 cup ricotta cheese
1/3 cup low-fat plain yogurt
1/3 cup granulated sugar
1/4 cup strong black
    coffee, cooled
1/2 teaspoon ground cinnamon
dash of vanilla extract

method

1 Grate the chocolate and set aside. Put the ricotta cheese, yogurt, and sugar in a food processor or blender and process until smooth. Transfer to a la bowl and beat in the coffee, cinnamon, vanilla extract, and grated chocolate.

2 Spoon the mixture into a freezerproof container and freeze for 1 1/2 hours, or until slushy. Remove from the freezer, turn into a bowl, and beat. Return to the container and freeze for 1 1/2 hours.

3 Repeat this beating and freezing process two more times. Keep in the freezer until 15 minutes before serving, then transfer to the refrigerator to soften slightly before serving. Serve in scoops, decorated w a little grated chocolate.

cappuccino ice cream

ingredients

serves 4

²/₃ cup whole milk
2½ cups heavy whipping cream
¼ cup finely ground fresh coffee
3 extra-large egg yolks
½ cup granulated sugar
unsweetened cocoa powder,
    for dusting
chocolate-coated coffee beans,
    to decorate

method

1 Pour the milk and 2 cups of the cream into a heavy saucepan, stir in the coffee, and bring almost to a boil. Remove from the heat, let steep for 5 minutes, then strain through a paper coffee filter or a strainer lined with cheesecloth.

2 Put the egg yolks and sugar in a large bowl and beat together until pale and the mixture leaves a trail when the beaters are lifted. Slowly add the milk mixture, stirring all the time with a wooden spoon. Strain the mixture into the rinsed-out pan or a double boiler and cook over low heat for 10–15 minutes, stirring all the time, until the mixture thickens enough to coat the back of the spoon. Do not let the mixture boil or it will curdle. Remove from the heat and let cool for at least 1 hour, stirring from time to time to prevent a skin from forming.

3 Churn the cold custard in an ice-cream maker, following the manufacturer's directions.

4 To serve, whip the remaining cream until it holds soft peaks. Scoop the ice cream into wide-brimmed coffee cups and smooth the tops. Spoon the whipped cream over the top of each and sprinkle with cocoa powder. Decorate with chocolate-coated coffee beans.

brown sugar mocha cream

ingredients

serves 4–6

1¼ cups heavy cream

1 teaspoon vanilla extract

2 cups fresh whole-wheat bread crumbs

⅓ cup firmly packed dark brown sugar

1 tablespoon instant coffee granules

2 tablespoons unsweetened cocoa powder

grated chocolate, to decorate (optional)

method

1 Whip the cream and vanilla extract in a large bowl until it is thick and holds soft peaks.

2 Mix the bread crumbs, sugar, coffee, and cocoa powder in another large bowl and layer the dry mixture with the whipped cream in serving glasses, ending with whipped cream. Sprinkle with grated chocolate if using.

3 Cover and let chill in the refrigerator for several hours or overnight.

cappuccino mousses

ingredients

serves 4

1 sheet gelatin
2 tablespoons instant coffee granules
1/4 cup water
1/3 cup superfine sugar or granulated sugar
1 1/4 cups heavy cream
1 extra-large egg white
1 tablespoon finely grated milk chocolate
4 chocolate-coated coffee beans, to decorate

method

1 Soak the gelatin in a bowl of cold water for 5 minute until soft. Put the coffee granules, water, and 2 tablespoons of the sugar into a small saucepan and heat gently until the coffee has dissolved.

2 Drain the softened gelatin, squeezing out any exces water, and add to the hot coffee. Stir gently, until th gelatin has dissolved, then let the mixture cool for 20 minutes.

3 Pour the cream into a bowl and whip until it holds s peaks. Remove 1/3 cup of the cream and reserve for decoration. Gently fold the coffee mixture into the remaining cream.

4 Beat the egg white in a clean, grease-free bowl unti forms soft peaks, then beat in the remaining sugar. Fold into the coffee cream and divide the mixture among four dessert glasses. Spoon the reserved whipped cream on top of the mousses.

5 Chill in the refrigerator for 1–2 hours, or until set. Sprinkle with the grated chocolate and decorate each mousse with a chocolate-coated coffee bean.

white chocolate tiramisu

ingredients

serves 4

16 ladyfingers
1 cup strong black coffee,
    cooled to room temperature
1/4 cup almond-flavored liqueur,
    such as amaretto
1 cup mascarpone cheese
1 1/4 cups heavy cream
3 tablespoons granulated sugar
4 ounces white chocolate, grated
1/4 cup toasted slivered almonds,
    to decorate

method

1 Break the ladyfingers into pieces and divide half of them equally among four serving glasses. Mix toge[ther] the coffee and liqueur in a small bowl, then pour ha[lf] the mixture over the ladyfingers in the glasses.

2 Beat the mascarpone, cream, sugar, and half of the chocolate in a bowl. Spread half the mixture over th[e] coffee-soaked ladyfingers, then arrange the remain[ing] ladyfingers on top. Pour the rest of the coffee mixt[ure] over the top layer, then spread with the remaining cream mixture. Sprinkle with the remaining chocola[te.]

3 Cover with plastic wrap and chill for at least 2 hours, or until required. Sprinkle with the slivered almonds before serving.

espresso crème brûlée

ingredients

serves 4

2 cups heavy cream

1 tablespoon instant espresso powder

4 extra-large egg yolks

¾ cup granulated sugar, plus extra for sprinkling

2 tablespoons coffee liqueur, such as Kahlúa

method

1 Preheat the oven to 225°F and put four shallow ovenproof white porcelain dishes on a baking sheet.

2 Put the cream in a small saucepan over medium-high heat and heat until small bubbles appear around the edges. Mix in the espresso powder, stirring until it dissolves, then remove the pan from the heat and let stand until completely cool.

3 Lightly beat the egg yolks in a bowl, then add the sugar and continue beating until thick and creamy.

4 Reheat the cream over medium-high heat until small bubbles appear around the edges. Stir the hot cream into the egg-yolk mixture, beating continuously. Stir in the coffee liqueur. Divide the custard mixture among the dishes and bake for 35–40 minutes, or until the custard wobbles slightly when you shake the dishes.

5 Remove the custards from the oven and let cool completely. Cover with plastic wrap and let chill in the refrigerator for at least 4 hours, but ideally overnight.

6 Before you are ready to serve, preheat the broiler to high. Sprinkle each custard with the sugar and put the dishes under the preheated broiler until the topping is golden and bubbling. Let cool for a few minutes before serving.

hot chocolate soufflé with coffee zabaglione

ingredients

serves 4–6

butter, for greasing

¼ cup granulated sugar, plus extra for coating

3 tablespoons cornstarch

1 cup milk

4 ounces semisweet chocolate, broken into pieces

4 eggs, separated

confectioners' sugar, for dusting

zabaglione

2 eggs, beaten

3 egg yolks

⅓ cup granulated sugar

4 teaspoons instant coffee granules

2 tablespoons brandy

method

1 Preheat the oven to 375°F. Grease a 1-quart soufflé di and coat with granulated sugar. To make the soufflé, put the cornstarch in a bowl. Add a little milk and stir until smooth. Pour the remaining milk into a heavy saucepan and add the chocolate. Heat gently until th chocolate has melted, then stir. Pour the chocolate m onto the cornstarch paste, stirring. Return to the pan and bring to a boil, stirring. Simmer for 1 minute. Remove from the heat and stir in the egg yolks, one a a time. Cover and cool slightly.

2 Put the egg whites in a large, clean bowl and beat un soft peaks form. Gradually beat in the granulated sug until stiff but not dry. Stir a little of the egg whites into the chocolate mixture, then carefully fold in the remainder. Pour into the prepared soufflé dish, then bake in the preheated oven for 40 minutes, or until it is well risen and wobbles slightly when shaken

3 Just before the soufflé is ready, make the coffee zabaglione. Put all the ingredients in a heavy saucepa over low heat and cook, beating continuously, until t mixture is thick and light. Dust a little confectioners' sugar over the soufflé and serve immediately, with the zabaglione.

irish cream cheesecake

ingredients

serves 8

vegetable oil, for oiling
6 ounces chocolate-chip cookies
4 tablespoons unsalted butter
crème fraîche or Greek-style yogurt
and fresh strawberries, to serve

filling

8 ounces semisweet chocolate,
broken into pieces
8 ounces milk chocolate,
broken into pieces
¼ cup granulated sugar
1½ cups cream cheese
2 cups heavy cream,
lightly whipped
2 tablespoons Irish cream liqueur
1 tablespooon strong black coffee

method

1 Line the bottom of an 8-inch round springform cake
pan with parchment paper and brush the sides with
Put the cookies in a plastic food bag and crush with
a rolling pin. Put the butter in a saucepan and heat
gently until melted. Stir in the crushed cookies. Press
into the bottom of the prepared cake pan and chill in
the refrigerator for 1 hour.

2 Put the semisweet chocolate and milk chocolate into
a heatproof bowl, set the bowl over a saucepan of
gently simmering water, and heat until melted. Cool.
Put the sugar and cream cheese in a bowl and beat
until smooth, then fold in the cream. Fold the melted
chocolate into the cream-cheese mixture, then stir in
the liqueur.

3 Spoon into the cake pan and smooth the surface with
a spatula. Let chill in the refrigerator for 2 hours, or u
firm. Transfer to a serving plate and cut into slices.
Serve with crème fraîche and sliced strawberries.

mocha creams

ingredients

serves 2–4

12 marshmallows
½ cup strong black coffee
2 ounces semisweet chocolate,
    finely chopped
    or grated
1¼ cups heavy cream

method

1 Put the marshmallows in a saucepan with the coffee and half the chocolate. Heat gently until melted. Remove the pan from the heat and allow to cool.

2 Whip the cream in a large bowl until thick and holds soft peaks, then gently stir in the coffee mixture.

3 Spoon into two to four serving bowls or dishes and sprinkle with the remaining chocolate. Chill in the refrigerator until ready to serve.

mocha fondue

ingredients

serves 4

8 ounces semisweet chocolate (at
    least 50 percent cocoa solids),
    broken into small pieces
½ cup heavy cream
1 tablespoon instant
    coffee granules
3 tablespoons coffee-flavored
    liqueur, such as Kahlúa

for the dippers

small sweet cookies,
    such as amaretti
plain or coffee-flavored marble
    cake or sponge cake,
    cut into bite-size pieces
whole seedless grapes
firm peaches or nectarines, pitted
    and sliced

method

1 Arrange the dippers decoratively on a serving platter
    or individual serving plates and set aside.

2 Put the chocolate in a heatproof bowl and set the bowl
    over a saucepan of gently simmering water, making
    sure that the bowl does not touch the water. Add the
    cream and coffee granules and heat, stirring, until
    melted and smooth. Remove from the heat and stir in
    the liqueur, then carefully pour the chocolate mixture
    into a warm fondue pot.

3 Using protective gloves, transfer the fondue pot to
    a lit tabletop burner. To serve, instruct your guests
    to spear the dippers with fondue forks and dip them
    into the fondue.

mochachino brownies

ingredients

makes 8–9

1 stick unsalted butter, plus extra
for greasing
4 ounces semisweet chocolate,
broken into pieces
2 tablespoons strong black coffee
1¼ cups granulated sugar
½ teaspoon ground cinnamon
3 eggs, beaten
⅔ cup all-purpose flour
⅓ cup milk chocolate chips
½ cup toasted walnuts, skinned
and chopped, plus extra
to decorate

white mocha sauce

½ cup heavy cream
3 ounces white chocolate,
broken into pieces
1 tablespoon strong black coffee

method

1 Preheat the oven to 350°F. Grease and line a 9-inch square baking pan.

2 Put the butter, chocolate. and coffee in a medium saucepan over low heat and stir until just melted and smooth. Cool slightly.

3 Beat in the sugar, cinnamon, and eggs. Beat in the flour, chocolate chips, and walnuts. Pour the batter into the prepared pan.

4 Bake in the oven for 30–35 minutes, until just firm but still moist inside. Cool in the pan, then cut into square or bars.

5 Meanwhile, make the sauce by putting all the ingredients in a small saucepan over low heat, stirring occasionally, until melted and smooth.

6 Put the brownies on individual plates and spoon the warm sauce on top. Decorate with chopped walnuts and serve.

raspberry dessert cake

ingredients

serves 8–10

2 sticks unsalted butter,
    plus extra for greasing
8 ounces semisweet chocolate,
    broken into pieces
1 tablespoon strong dark coffee
5 eggs
½ cup granulated sugar
½ cup all-purpose flour
1 teaspoon ground cinnamon
1½ cups fresh raspberries,
    plus extra to serve
confectioners' sugar, for dusting
whipped cream, to serve

method

1 Preheat the oven to 325°F. Grease a 9-inch cake pan
and line the bottom with parchment paper. Put the
chocolate, butter, and coffee in a heatproof bowl, se
the bowl over a saucepan of gently simmering wate
and heat until melted. Remove from the heat and st
then allow to cool slightly.

2 Beat the eggs and sugar in a separate bowl until pa
and thick. Gently fold the chocolate mixture into the
egg and sugar mixture.

3 Sift the flour and cinnamon into another bowl, then
fold into the chocolate mixture. Pour into the prepa
pan and sprinkle the raspberries evenly over the top

4 Bake in the preheated oven for about 35–45 minutes,
until the cake is well risen and springy to the touch.
Allow to cool in the pan for 15 minutes before turning
out onto a large serving plate. Dust with confectioner
sugar before serving with fresh raspberries and
whipped cream.

mocha coconut clusters

ingredients

makes 30

4 ounces milk chocolate,
broken into small pieces

2 tablespoons butter

1 teaspoon instant coffee granules

½ cup shredded unsweetened
dried coconut

method

1 Line two to three baking sheets with parchment pap
Put the chocolate and butter in a heatproof bowl, se
the bowl over a saucepan of gently simmering water
and heat, stirring, until melted and smooth. Remove
the bowl from the heat.

2 Stir the coffee granules into the chocolate until
dissolved, then stir in the coconut.

3 Put heaping teaspoons of the mixture on the prepar
baking sheets, cover, and chill in the refrigerator unt
set. To serve, put each cluster in a paper candy cup.

mocha pecan tarts

ingredients

serves 4

1 cup all-purpose flour,
    plus extra for dusting
6 tablespoons unsalted butter,
    chilled and diced
2 tablespoons confectioners' sugar
1 egg yolk

filling

¼ cup firmly packed light
    brown sugar
4 tablespoons butter
1½ teaspoons instant
    coffee granules
2 ounces semisweet chocolate,
    finely chopped
3 tablespoons maple syrup
2 tablespoons light corn syrup
2 extra-large eggs, beaten
1 cup pecans

method

1 Put the flour, butter, and confectioners' sugar into a food processor or blender. Process for a few seconds make fine crumbs. With the machine running, add th egg yolk and process until the mixture begins to bin together. Turn out onto a lightly floured surface and knead gently until smooth. Wrap in plastic wrap and chill in the refrigerator for 30 minutes.

2 Divide the dough into four pieces. Roll out on a lightly floured surface and use to line four 4-inch loose-botton fluted mini tart pans. Prick the bottoms with a fork and chill for 1 hour. Meanwhile, preheat the oven to 375°F. Place a baking sheet in the oven.

3 To make the filling, put the sugar, butter, and coffee granules into a small saucepan and heat gently, stirr until the sugar and coffee have dissolved. Remove fr the heat, add the chocolate, and stir until melted. Le cool for 5 minutes, then beat in the maple syrup, co syrup, and eggs.

4 Chop two-thirds of the nuts and stir into the mixture Divide the mixture among the pastry shells and top with the remaining nuts. Place the tarts on the preheated baking sheet and bake for 20–25 minute: or until the pastry is golden and the filling has just se Serve warm or cold.

hot espresso cakes

ingredients

serves 6

oil or melted butter, for greasing
1⅓ cups all-purpose flour
1 tablespoon baking powder
1 tablespoon unsweetened
    cocoa powder
1½ sticks unsalted butter, softened
¾ cup firmly packed light
    brown sugar
3 eggs, beaten
1 teaspoon vanilla extract
3 tablespoons strong espresso
    coffee, cooled
brown sugar crystals, to serve

sauce

1 tablespoon cornstarch
1 cup strong espresso coffee
½ cup light cream
3 tablespoons packed light
    brown sugar

method

1 Preheat the oven to 350°F. Grease and line a 7 x 11-inc
   rectangular cake pan.

2 Sift the flour, baking powder, and cocoa into a large
   bowl and add the butter, sugar, eggs, and vanilla
   extract. Beat well until the batter is smooth, then
   beat in the coffee.

3 Spoon the batter into the prepared pan and smooth
   the surface with a spatula. Bake in the preheated ove
   for 30–35 minutes, or until the cake has risen and is
   firm and golden brown.

4 Meanwhile, to make the sauce, mix the cornstarch w
   2 tablespoons of the coffee, then add to a saucepan
   with the remaining coffee, the cream, and sugar. Hea
   gently, stirring, until boiling, then reduce the heat an
   stir for 2 minutes, or until slightly thickened.

5 Using a 3½-inch plain cookie cutter, stamp out six
   circles from the cake (trimmings can be eaten cold).
   Place on warm serving plates, spoon the sauce over
   the top, and sprinkle each with a few sugar crystals.

espresso mint chocolate truffles

ingredients

makes 24

8 ounces semisweet chocolate,
    broken into pieces

4 tablespoons unsalted butter

⅔ cup heavy cream

2 tablespoons espresso
    coffee, cooled

few drops peppermint extract

1–2 tablespoons unsweetened
    cocoa powder

method

1 Put the chocolate and butter into a heatproof bowl,
   the bowl over a saucepan of gently simmering wate
   and heat until melted. Remove from the heat and sti
   until smooth. Cool for 5 minutes.

2 Mix the cream, coffee, and peppermint extract and s
   into the chocolate mixture. Cool for 20–30 minutes,
   stirring occasionally, then chill in the refrigerator for
   2–3 hours, until firm enough to shape.

3 Sift the cocoa powder onto a flat plate. Divide and
   shape the chocolate mixture into 24 truffles, rolling
   lightly between the palms of your hands. Roll each
   truffle in cocoa powder to coat. Chill in the refrigerat
   for 1–2 hours, until firm.

variation

For a delicious nutty coating, roll the truffles in 1 cup of
finely chopped walnuts, pecans, or pistachios instead
of cocoa powder.

savory recipes

coffee-braised beef pot roast

ingredients

serves 4

2¼-pound beef brisket
salt and pepper
1 tablespoon butter
2 tablespoons sunflower oil
2 onions, cut into wedges
5 carrots, cut into chunks
2 parsnips, cut into chunks
1¼ cups strong black coffee, cooled
1 cup beef stock
2 tablespoons tomato paste
2 tablespoons Worcestershire sauce
1 tablespoon balsamic vinegar
few fresh thyme sprigs,
    plus extra to garnish
2 tablespoons cornstarch
2–3 tablespoons water
boiled potatoes, to serve

method

1 Preheat the oven to 325°F. Season the beef with salt and pepper.

2 Heat half the butter and half the oil in a large skillet. Add the beef and cook over high heat for a few minutes, until browned all over. Transfer to a large casserole dish or Dutch oven.

3 Add the remaining butter and oil to the skillet, then add the onions, carrots, and parsnips and sauté for 5 minutes. Stir in the coffee, stock, tomato paste, Worcestershire sauce, and vinegar and bring to a bo

4 Spoon the vegetables and liquid around the beef. Lightly season with salt and pepper and add the thyr Cover and cook in the preheated oven for 2¼ hours.

5 Remove the casserole from the oven. Blend the cornstarch to a paste with the water and stir into the hot liquid. Return the casserole to the oven, cover, an cook for an additional 30–40 minutes, until the beef a vegetables are tender and the liquid has thickened.

6 Remove the beef from the casserole dish and carve into thick slices. Divide the vegetables and gravy among four shallow serving bowls, top with the beef, and garnish with thyme sprigs. Serve with boiled potatoes.

blackened coffee rib-eye steaks

ingredients

serves 2

2 teaspoons finely ground espresso coffee

2 teaspoons dried oregano

1 teaspoon packed light brown sugar

1 teaspoon pepper

½ teaspoon sea salt

2 rib-eye steaks (at room temperature), each about 8 ounces and about 1 inch thick

1 tablespoon olive oil

2 tablespoons butter

arugula and watercress salad, to serve

fresh Parmesan cheese shavings, to garnish

method

1 Mix the coffee, oregano, sugar, pepper, and salt and spread on a shallow plate. Dip each side of the steak the mixture to coat.

2 Heat the oil and butter in a large, heavy skillet until sizzling. Add the steaks and cook on each side for 2–3 minutes, until black on the outside for medium-rare. Increase the cooking time slightly for well-done steaks.

3 Transfer the steaks to a warm plate. Cover with aluminum foil and allow to rest in a warm place for 10 minutes.

4 To serve, slice each steak into five to six slices and pl on warm serving plates. Pour any meat juices over th steak and serve with an arugula and watercress salac garnished with Parmesan cheese shavings.

beef in coffee sauce

ingredients

serves 6

1/4 cup sunflower oil
3 pounds eye of round steak
    or chuck steak, cut into
    1-inch cubes
4 onions, sliced
1 garlic clove, finely chopped
1/3 cup all-purpose flour
1 1/4 cups red wine
pinch of dried oregano
1 small fresh rosemary sprig
2 cups black coffee
salt and pepper
fresh marjoram sprigs, to garnish
mashed sweet potatoes, to serve

method

1 Heat the oil in a large, deep skillet. Add the steak cub
and cook over medium heat, stirring frequently, for
8–10 minutes, until evenly browned. Using a slotted
spoon, transfer to a casserole dish. Preheat the oven
to 325°F.

2 Add the onions and garlic to the skillet, reduce the
heat, and cook, stirring occasionally, for 10 minutes,
until softened and just beginning to brown. Stir
in the flour and cook, stirring continuously, for
1 minute. Gradually stir in the wine, a little at a time.
Add the oregano and rosemary, season with salt
and pepper, pour in the coffee, and bring to a boil,
stirring continuously.

3 Transfer the mixture to the casserole dish. Cover and
cook in the preheated oven for 2–2 1/4 hours, until the
meat is tender. Remove and discard the rosemary sp
Taste and adjust the seasoning, adding salt and pep
if needed. Garnish with marjoram sprigs and serve
immediately with mashed sweet potatoes.

cowboy coffee burgers

ingredients

serves 4

1 tablespoon instant coffee granules, finely ground

2 teaspoons packed light brown sugar

1 teaspoon salt

¼ teaspoon pepper

1 pound ground chuck beef

1 small onion, grated

1 egg yolk

olive oil, for brushing

to serve

4 hamburger buns

¼ cup mayonnaise

1 teaspoon smooth mustard

peppery salad greens

4 beefsteak tomato slices

method

1 Put the coffee, sugar, salt, and pepper into a large bo and mix. Add the beef, onion, and egg yolk and mix with your hands until thoroughly combined. Divide t mixture into four portions and shape each into a pat

2 Preheat a ridged grill pan or cast-iron skillet. Lightly brush the patties with oil and cook for 6–8 minutes c each side, or until cooked through. Alternatively, coo under a hot broiler.

3 To serve, halve and lightly toast the burger buns. Mix the mayonnaise and mustard. Put some salad greens tomato slice, and a burger on top of four bun halves. Add a dollop of mustard-mayonnaise and top with t remaining bun halves. Serve immediately.

coffee barbecue-glazed spareribs

ingredients

serves 4

2 racks pork spareribs,
    about 1¾ pounds
3 tablespoons instant coffee
    granules, dissolved in
    ⅓ cup hot water
⅓ cup ketchup
2 tablespoons vegetable oil
3 tablespoons Worcestershire sauce
3 tablespoons smooth
    mango chutney
salt and pepper
salad, to serve

method

1 Put the racks of ribs into a large saucepan and cover with water. Bring to a boil, skim off any scum from the surface, then simmer for 25 minutes.

2 Lift the ribs out of the water and place on a metal rack set over a large roasting pan. Preheat the oven to 375°F.

3 Put the coffee, ketchup, oil, Worcestershire sauce, and chutney into a bowl and mix together. Season with salt and pepper.

4 Liberally brush the coffee glaze over the racks of ribs. Roast in the preheated oven for 45 minutes, basting occasionally, until the glaze is sticky and lightly charred in places and the ribs are tender. Serve immediately with salad.

coffee-glazed ham

ingredients

serves 10

4½-pound Virginia or other
country ham
1 onion, quartered
few black peppercorns
1 bay leaf
½ cup cold strong black coffee
½ cup raw brown sugar
⅓ cup honey
2 tablespoons whole-grain
mustard
1 tablespoon white-wine vinegar
bay leaves, to garnish

method

1 Put the ham into a large, deep saucepan and cover
with cold water. Add the onion, peppercorns, and bay
leaf and bring to a boil. Reduce the heat to simmering
cover, and cook for 1½ hours. Add more boiling water
if needed.

2 Meanwhile, put the coffee, sugar, honey, mustard, and
vinegar into a small saucepan. Bring to a boil, then
simmer for 10–15 minutes, until syrupy. Set aside.

3 Remove the ham from the liquid and allow to cool for
10 minutes, then cut away the skin, leaving a thin layer
of fat. Score the fat into diamonds with the tip of a
knife. Line a roasting pan with aluminum foil and place
the ham in the pan. Preheat the oven to 350°F.

4 Pour two-thirds of the coffee glaze over the ham. Roast
in the preheated oven for 25 minutes, then pour the
remaining glaze over the ham. Roast for an additional
35–45 minutes, basting 2–3 times, until the glaze is
dark golden and caramelized at the edges.

5 Cover the ham and rest it in a warm place for
15 minutes before carving. Pour all the juices from
the lined roasting pan into a small pitcher. Garnish the
ham with the bay leaves and serve with the juice.

coffee-crusted lamb cutlets

ingredients

serves 2

3 garlic cloves, crushed

1 tablespoon instant coffee granules

2 teaspoons pepper

½ teaspoon sea salt

2 thick lamb cutlets, about 6 ounces each

1 tablespoon sunflower oil

mint sprigs, to garnish

to serve

sautéed or boiled new potatoes

fresh, cooked peas and beans

method

1 Grind the crushed garlic, coffee, pepper, and salt into a coarse paste using a mortar and pestle. Spread the paste over both sides of each lamb cutlet. Place on a plate, cover, and let marinate in the refrigerator for 1–2 hours.

2 Preheat the oven to 400°F.

3 Heat the oil in a skillet until almost smoking. Add the meat and sear in the hot oil, turning, until browned all over.

4 Transfer to a shallow roasting pan and cook in the preheated oven for 15–20 minutes, depending on the thickness of the cutlets and how well done you would like the meat. Remove from the oven, cover with aluminum foil, and allow to rest in a warm place for 10 minutes.

5 Thickly slice each cutlet and arrange on warm serving plates. Garnish with mint and serve immediately with potatoes and freshly cooked peas and beans.

coffee-marinated chicken drumsticks

ingredients

serves 4

8 large chicken drumsticks
⅔ cup strong black coffee, cooled
3 tablespoons honey
3 tablespoons sweet chili sauce
1 tablespoon dark soy sauce
salt and pepper
fries and oven-roasted tomatoes
    on the vine, to serve

method

1 Place the drumsticks in a shallow, nonmetallic dish. M the coffee, honey, chili sauce, and soy sauce and pou the marinade over the drumsticks.

2 Lightly season with salt and pepper, cover, and marinate at room temperature for 1–2 hours.

3 Preheat the oven to 400°F. Remove the drumsticks fro the marinade and place in a roasting pan. Roast in th preheated oven for 20 minutes. Meanwhile, pour the marinade into a small saucepan, bring to a boil, then reduce the heat and simmer gently for 15 minutes, until syrupy.

4 Remove the pan from the oven and pour the hot marinade all over the drumsticks. Return to the oven and roast, basting occasionally, for an additiona 20–25 minutes, or until they are cooked through and golden brown. Serve hot or cold with fries and oven-roasted tomatoes on the vine.

turkey stir-fry with spiced coffee glaze

ingredients

serves 4

1 pound turkey breast, sliced into thin strips

1 teaspoon finely grated fresh ginger

2 garlic cloves, crushed

1 teaspoon five-spice seasoning

4 teaspoons sesame oil

¼ cup strong black coffee, cooled

¼ cup teriyaki sauce

2 tablespoons honey

2 tablespoons rice-wine vinegar

2 teaspoons cornstarch

6 scallions, trimmed and sliced

1 red bell pepper, seeded and thinly sliced

1 yellow bell pepper, seeded and thinly sliced

salt and pepper

boiled egg noodles, to serve

method

1 Place the turkey in a shallow, nonmetallic bowl and add the ginger, garlic, five-spice seasoning, and half the oil. Stir well, then cover and marinate in the refrigerator for 1 hour.

2 Mix the coffee, teriyaki sauce, honey, vinegar, and cornstarch in a small bowl. Cover and set aside.

3 Heat the remaining oil in a large wok until almost smoking. Remove the turkey from the marinade, add to the wok, and stir-fry over high heat for 3–4 minutes until brown. Add the scallions, red bell pepper, and yellow bell pepper and stir-fry for an additional 1–2 minutes.

4 Pour in the coffee mixture and continue stir-frying for 1–2 minutes, until the sauce has thickened and coated the turkey and vegetables. Season with salt and pepper and serve with noodles.

chili espresso rub

ingredients

makes about ⅓ cup

2 tablespoons packed dark
    brown sugar
1 tablespoon ground
    espresso coffee
1 tablespoon ground coriander
2 teaspoons ground cumin
1 teaspoons ground ginger
1–2 teaspoons crushed red pepper
    or chili powder
salt and pepper

method

1 Mix all the ingredients in a small bowl until thoroughl
    combined.

2 Rub the mixture thoroughly into meat, poultry, fish, o
    seafood up to 6 hours before cooking.

3 Put in a shallow dish, cover tightly, and chill in the
    refrigerator until required.

chili with coffee

ingredients

serves 4

1 tablespoon olive oil
1 red onion, chopped
2 garlic cloves, chopped
1 pound ground round beef
1½ tablespoons hot chili powder
½ teaspoon ground cumin
1 teaspoon dried oregano
1 cup strong black coffee, cooled
1 (14½-ounce) can diced tomatoes
2 tablespoons tomato paste
1 teaspoon sugar
1 cup canned red kidney beans,
    drained and rinsed
salt and pepper

to serve
sour cream
chopped fresh green chile
tortilla chips

method

1 Heat the oil in a large, deep skillet, add the onion and garlic, and sauté for 5 minutes. Add the beef and cook over high heat for 8–10 minutes, stirring frequently, until browned all over.

2 Stir in the chili powder, cumin, and oregano and cook for 1 minute, then add the coffee, diced tomatoes, tomato paste, and sugar. Season with salt and pepper and stir. Add the beans and cook, uncovered, for an additional 10–15 minutes.

3 Spoon into warm bowls, top with spoonfuls of sour cream and some chopped chile, and serve immediately with tortilla chips.

coffee & walnut bread

ingredients

makes 1 loaf

vegetable oil, for greasing
1½ cups whole-wheat bread flour,
    plus extra for dusting
1⅔ cups white bread flour
1 teaspoon salt
1 teaspoon active dry yeast
¾ cup coarsely chopped walnuts
1¼ cups lukewarm water
1 tablespoon instant
    coffee granules
1 tablespoon olive oil
1 tablespoon honey

method

1 Grease a baking sheet. Put the whole-wheat flour, white flour, salt, yeast, and walnuts into a large bowl and mix. Put the water, coffee, olive oil, and honey into a separate bowl and mix. Make a well in the center of the flour mixture and pour in the liquid. Mix with a kn to make a soft, sticky dough.

2 Turn out the dough onto a floured surface and knead for 5–7 minutes, until smooth and elastic. Put the dough into a bowl, cover with oiled plastic wrap, and allow to rest in a warm place for about 1 hour, or until doubled in size.

3 Turn out the dough onto a floured surface and lightly knead for 1 minute. Shape into an 8-inch-long oval an place on the prepared baking sheet. Dust the top of the loaf with whole-wheat flour and slash a curve along the top of the loaf (just off center). Allow to res in a warm place for 40–50 minutes, or until doubled i size. Meanwhile, preheat the oven to 400°F.

4 Bake in the preheated oven for 18–20 minutes, or until golden brown and the bottom sounds hollow when tapped with your knuckles. Transfer the bread to a wire rack to cool.

drinks

s'mores coffee & chocolate cup

ingredients

serves 4

2½ cups milk
½ cup strong black coffee
8 ounces milk chocolate or
    semisweet chocolate
    (or a mixture), finely chopped
24 pink and white marshmallows
1 tablespoon store-bought
    chocolate sauce, warmed
2 teaspoons finely grated
    semisweet chocolate

method

1 Put the milk and coffee into a saucepan and heat over medium heat until almost boiling. Remove from the heat and stir in the chopped chocolate. Beat briskly until the chocolate has melted.

2 Return to the heat and simmer gently for 1–2 minute. Preheat the broiler to high. Divide the hot chocolate among four coffee cups or mugs and top with the marshmallows. Place the cups under the preheated broiler for about 1 minute, until the marshmallows begin to brown and melt.

3 Drizzle the chocolate sauce over the tops and sprinkl with the grated chocolate. Serve immediately.

cinnamon mocha

ingredients

serves 6

8 ounces milk chocolate,
    broken into pieces
¾ cup light cream
4 cups freshly brewed coffee
1 teaspoon ground cinnamon,
    plus extra to decorate

to serve
whipped cream
marbled chocolate curls

method

1 Put the chocolate in a large, heatproof bowl set over
  a saucepan of gently simmering water. Add the light
  cream and stir until the chocolate has melted and the
  mixture is smooth.

2 Pour in the coffee, add the cinnamon, and beat until
  foamy. If serving hot, pour into six heatproof glasses
  or mugs, top with whipped cream, a sprinkling
  of cinnamon, and the chocolate curls, and serve
  immediately. If serving cold, remove the bowl from
  the heat and allow to cool, then chill in the refrigerator
  until required. Pour into six glasses or mugs, top with
  whipped cream, a sprinkling of cinnamon, and the
  chocolate curls, and serve.

mocha whip

ingredients

serves 2

1 cup milk
¼ cup light cream
1 tablespoon packed brown sugar
2 tablespoons unsweetened
    cocoa powder
1 tablespoon coffee syrup or
    instant coffee powder
6 ice cubes

to serve
whipped cream
grated chocolate

method

1 Put the milk, light cream, and sugar into a food processor or blender and process gently until combined.

2 Add the cocoa powder and coffee syrup or powder and process well, then add the ice cubes and process until smooth.

3 Divide the mixture between two glasses. Top with whipped cream, sprinkle with the grated chocolate, and serve.

hot caramel latte

ingredients

serves 2

¼ cup granulated sugar
⅓ cup water
1¼ cups milk
½ cup hot espresso coffee

method

1 To make the caramel, put the sugar and 2 tablespoon of the water into a small, heavy saucepan. Heat gently until the sugar dissolves, then boil rapidly for 4–5 minutes, without stirring, until the mixture turns to a golden caramel.

2 Remove from the heat and carefully pour in the remaining water. Stir until the caramel dissolves, then return the pan to the heat and simmer for an additional 3–4 minutes, until syrupy.

3 Put the milk into a separate saucepan and heat over medium heat until almost boiling. Remove from the heat, pour in the coffee and almost all the caramel sauce, and whisk until frothy. Divide between two ta latte glasses.

4 Drizzle the remaining caramel sauce over the top an serve immediately.

variation

For a festive winter latte, substitute 2 tablespoons of gingerbread-flavored syrup (available in some supermarkets and online) for the caramel. Omit steps 1, 2, and 4.

coconut coffee cocktail

ingredients

serves 1

1 tablespoon coconut liqueur
1 tablespoon coffee liqueur
1 tablespoon brandy
1 cup freshly brewed hot coffee
whipped cream, to serve

method

1 Mix the liqueurs and brandy in a heatproof glass or mug.

2 Pour in the fresh coffee and top with a spoonful of whipped cream.

amaretto coffee

ingredients

serves 1

2 tablespoons amaretto

sugar, to taste

1 cup freshly made strong
    black coffee

1–2 tablespoons heavy cream

method

1 Put the amaretto into a warm heatproof glass and
    add sugar to taste.

2 Pour in the coffee and stir.

3 When the sugar has completely dissolved, slowly
    pour in the cream over the back of a spoon so that
    it floats on top.

4 Don't stir—drink the coffee through the cream.

hungarian coffee

ingredients

serves 1

2 tablespoons brandy
sugar, to taste
1 cup freshly made strong
    black coffee
1 tablespoon grated chocolate
whipped cream, to serve
cinnamon stick, to serve

method

1 Put the brandy into a warm heatproof glass and add sugar to taste.

2 Pour in the coffee and grated chocolate and stir.

3 When the sugar has completely dissolved and the chocolate has melted, top with the whipped cream and decorate with the cinnamon stick.

4 Don't stir—drink the coffee through the cream.

irish coffee

ingredients

serves 1

2 tablespoons Irish whiskey
sugar, to taste
1 cup freshly made strong
   black coffee
2–4 tablespoons heavy cream

method

1 Put the whiskey into a warm heatproof glass and add sugar to taste.

2 Pour in the coffee and stir.

3 When the sugar has completely dissolved, slowly pour in the cream over the back of a spoon so that it floats on top.

4 Don't stir—drink the coffee through the cream.

coffee hazelnut soda

ingredients

serves 2

3 tablespoons instant
   coffee granules
1 cup boiling water
½ cup sparkling water
1 tablespoon hazelnut syrup
2 tablespoons brown sugar
6 ice cubes
slices of lime, to serve

method

1 Make the instant coffee with the water, cool to room temperature, cover with plastic wrap, and chill in the refrigerator for 45 minutes.

2 Pour the mixture into a food processor or blender, add the sparkling water, hazelnut syrup, and sugar, and process well. Add the ice cubes and process until smooth.

3 Divide the mixture between two glasses, decorate the rims with slices of fresh lime, and serve.

rum espresso with whipped cream

ingredients

serves 4

⅔ cup heavy cream
1¼ cups hot espresso coffee
1 tablespoon rum
2 teaspoons raw sugar,
    plus extra for sprinkling

method

1 Pour the heavy cream into a bowl and whip until it holds soft peaks.

2 Mix the coffee, rum, and sugar in a liquid measuring cup and pour into four small heatproof glasses or coffee cups.

3 Gently drop spoonfuls of the cream into the coffee. Sprinkle with a little extra sugar and serve immediatel

coffee & cinnamon eggnog

ingredients

serves 4

2 cups milk
²/₃ cup strong black coffee
1 cinnamon stick
2 extra-large eggs
¹/₃ cup granulated sugar
¹/₂ cup heavy cream
2 teaspoons ground cinnamon

method

1 Put the milk, coffee, and cinnamon stick into a saucepan and heat over medium heat until almost boiling. Cool for 5 minutes, then remove and discard the cinnamon stick.

2 Put the eggs and sugar into a bowl and beat until pale and thick. Gradually beat in the milk and coffee mixture. Return to the pan and heat gently, stirring all the time, until just thickened. Cool for 30 minutes.

3 Put the cream into a bowl and whip until it holds soft peaks. Gently fold the cream into the egg mixture. Divide among four glasses, sprinkle with ground cinnamon, and serve immediately, or chill for 1–2 hours in the refrigerator before serving.

midnight cowboy

ingredients

serves 1

2 tablespoons brandy
1 tablespoon coffee liqueur
1 tablespoon heavy cream, chilled
3 ice cubes, crushed
cola

method

1 Slowly mix the brandy, coffee liqueur, cream, and crushed ice in a blender until frothy.

2 Pour into a chilled glass. Top up with cola.

fuzzy martini

ingredients

serves 1

4 tablespoons vanilla vodka
1 tablespoon coffee vodka
1 teaspoon peach schnapps
3 ice cubes, crushed
peach slice, to decorate

method

1 Shake the vanilla vodka, coffee vodka, and peach schnapps over crushed ice until well chilled.

2 Strain into a chilled cocktail glass and decorate with the peach slice.

black russian

ingredients

serves 1

cracked ice cubes
4 tablespoons vodka
2 tablespoons coffee liqueur

method

1 Fill a lowball glass halfway with cracked ice.

2 Pour the vodka and coffee liqueur over the ice and stir to mix.

iced coffee with cream

ingredients

serves 2

1¾ cups boiling water
2 tablespoons instant
   coffee powder
2 tablespoons packed brown sugar
6 ice cubes, crushed

to decorate
light cream
whole coffee beans

method

1 Use the water and coffee powder to brew some hot coffee, then allow it to cool to room temperature. Cov with plastic wrap and chill in the refrigerator for at lea 45 minutes.

2 When the coffee has chilled, pour it into a food processor or blender. Add the sugar and process until well mixed. Add the crushed ice and process again until smooth.

3 Divide the mixture between two glasses. Float light cream on the top, decorate with the whole coffee beans, and serve.

sweet milk coffee

ingredients

serves 6

6 tablespoons canned sweetened
    condensed milk, or to taste
6 hot double espressos or
    strong-brewed Thai coffees
ice cubes, to serve (optional)

method

1 Put a tablespoon of condensed milk (or more to taste)
in each of six cups. Pour a hot double shot of espresso
into each cup and stir.

2 For iced coffee, fill six tall glasses halfway with ice
cubes. Pour a cup of stirred espresso with condensed
milk over the ice in each glass.

banana & coffee milkshake

ingredients

serves 2

1¼ cups milk
¼ cup instant coffee powder
2 scoops vanilla ice cream
2 bananas, sliced and frozen

method

1 Pour the milk into a food processor or blender, add the coffee powder, and process gently until mixed. Add half of the ice cream and process gently, then add the remaining ice cream and process until well mixed.

2 When the mixture is thoroughly blended, add the bananas and process until smooth.

3 Divide the mixture between two glasses and serve.

tex-mex coffee

ingredients

serves 1

1 teaspoon packed light brown
    sugar, or to taste
2 tablespoons Kahlúa or Tia Maria
1 tablespoon gold tequila
⅔ cup hot black coffee
1–2 tablespoons heavy cream
grated semisweet chocolate,
    to decorate

method

1 Put the sugar, Kahlúa, and tequila in a warm heatproof
    glass with a handle. Add the hot coffee
    and stir until the sugar has dissolved.

2 Hold a teaspoon, back uppermost, just touching the
    surface of the coffee. Carefully pour the cream over
    the back of the spoon so that it floats on the surface.

3 Sprinkle with grated chocolate and serve immediately

espresso galliano

ingredients

serves 1

4 tablespoons Galliano

sugar, to taste

⅔ cup freshly made strong black coffee

splash orange or lemon juice

orange zest strip, to decorate

method

1 Put the Galliano into a warm heatproof glass and add sugar to taste.

2 Pour in the coffee and orange juice and stir until the sugar has completely dissolved.

3 Decorate with the orange zest.

mocha milkshake

ingredients

serves 2

½ cup cold black coffee
1 tablespoon granulated sugar
⅔ cup milk
5 large scoops chocolate ice cream
2 tablespoons store-bought
    chocolate sauce
whipped cream, to serve

method

1 Put the coffee, sugar, and milk into a blender or food processor and process for a few seconds until frothy. Add the ice cream and blend for an additional 30 seconds.

2 Put the chocolate sauce into a paper pastry bag. Snip off the end and pipe half the sauce around the inside of two chilled, tall milkshake glasses.

3 Pour the milkshake into the glasses. Top with swirls of cream and drizzle with the remaining chocolate sauce. Serve immediately.

index